Literacy Teacher Preparation

Ten Truths Teacher Educators Need to Know

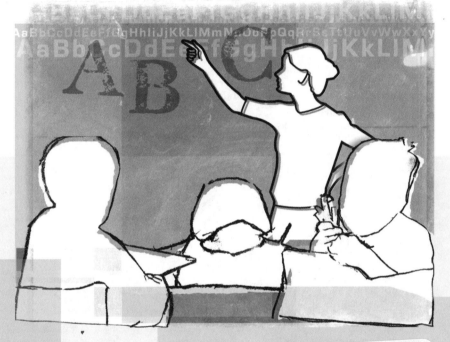

W9-BUQ-090

Susan Davis Lenski
Portland State University
Portland, Oregon, USA

Dana L. Grisham
San Diego State University
San Diego, California, USA
and
Center for the Advancement of Reading
California State University Office of the Chancellor
Sacramento, California, USA

Linda S. Wold
Loyola University Chicago
Chicago, Illinois, USA

EDITORS

INTERNATIONAL
Reading Association
800 BARKSDALE ROAD, PO BOX 8139
NEWARK, DE 19714-8139, USA
www.reading.org

The International Reading Association attempts, through its publications, to provide a forum for a wide spectrum of opinions on reading. This policy permits divergent viewpoints without implying the endorsement of the Association.

Director of Publications   Dan Mangan
Editorial Director, Books and Special Projects   Teresa Curto
Managing Editor, Books   Shannon T. Fortner
Acquisitions and Developmental Editor   Corinne M. Mooney
Associate Editor   Charlene M. Nichols
Associate Editor   Elizabeth C. Hunt
Production Editor   Amy Messick
Books and Inventory Assistant   Rebecca A. Zell
Permissions Editor   Janet S. Parrack
Assistant Permissions Editor   Tyanna L. Collins
Production Department Manager   Iona Muscella
Supervisor, Electronic Publishing   Anette Schütz
Senior Electronic Publishing Specialist   R. Lynn Harrison
Electronic Publishing Specialist   Lisa M. Kochel
Proofreader   Stacey Lynn Sharp

Project Editor   Amy Messick

Cover   Design, Linda Steere; Photo, Photodisc Illustration/Getty Images

Library of Congress Cataloging-in-Publication Data
Lenski, Susan Davis, 1951-
  Literacy teacher preparation : ten truths teacher educators need to know / Susan Davis Lenski, Dana L. Grisham, Linda S. Wold.
     p. cm.
  Includes bibliographical references and index.
  ISBN 0-87207-588-5
  1. Reading teachers--Training of. 2. Literacy. I. Grisham, Dana L., 1945- II. Wold, Linda S., 1949- III. Title.
  LB2844.1.R4L463 2005
  428.4'071--dc22
                                                              2005021195

First and foremost, we dedicate this book to the children who attend our schools across the United States. These children are the future and they deserve the finest education we can provide.

Because we are teacher educators, we dedicate this book also to the teachers we prepare. They deserve the best preparation that we can provide in order to capably serve their students. Teaching is service to our communities. It does not pay particularly well. It is not glamorous or high-status work, but it is one of the most important jobs any individual can undertake. The miracle is that intelligent and dedicated individuals enter the teaching profession every day with the resolve to make a difference in children's lives.

Finally, we dedicate this book to our many colleagues—the teacher educators in colleges and universities who labor diligently to provide research-based, substantive, and effective beginning teacher preparation and professional development education to the teaching field. We hope this book situates teacher educators in that tradition of excellence and service that we all seek to achieve.

CONTENTS

Problem or Solution?
Literacy Teacher Preparation
in the 21st Century

DANA L. GRISHAM

Many divisive issues exist in teacher preparation today. Researchers, policymakers, pundits, and even teacher educators themselves have written extensively about the controversial and contentious areas that the public perceives as needing reform, renewal, or both. The history of teacher preparation in the United States is one of public ownership and oversight. Every citizen has experience in education, stories about what education used to be like in the "good old days," and opinions about what education should be like today. Unlike medicine or engineering, most people consider education and schooling to be something that they know well and they usually have some fairly definite ideas about how they should be accomplished. Among the topics that have come under public scrutiny in the last quarter of the 20th century and the first several years of the 21st century is this very partial list: program quality, diversity, teacher characteristics, growth and new programs, resources, technology, and accountability.

Many of the listed topics are related, and different decades have seen different emphases on them, but throughout the years, literacy education has been an enduring focus of public scrutiny. We, the generations who have watched the general progress of society across two centuries, like to think that our times have been some of the most turbulent in history. Bruce (2002) argues that although our current era has seen momentous changes, such changes are not unprecedented but have had many precursors, most notably the dramatic impact on society of the discovery of electricity. Bruce makes the point that in the turning of the 19th century, we saw a greater change in society than we did in the turning of the 20th century. Regardless of which change was more tumultuous, the changes we have recently experienced are considerable and, to many, troubling.

Although society may change rapidly, society's conceptions of education change slowly, and the public characteristically perceives education as needing reform. Bruce notes, "The idea of 'crisis' has been a recurring theme in writings about American education" (p. 11). Berliner, Bell, and Biddle (1996) provide a number of statistically supported arguments for why the "crisis" in education is manufactured rather than real. Nevertheless, the crisis in U.S. education is part of the public's perception, and literacy education occupies a central position in current plans for reform and renewal.

It was partially in response to an acrimonious climate in literacy teacher preparation that a group of literacy teacher educators and researchers, members of the National Reading Conference (NRC), formed the Teacher Education Research Study Group (TERSG) in 1993. Members of TERSG met early each morning during the NRC's annual convention to discuss topics of interest, share experiences, and plan collaborative research for the following year.

At the TERSG meetings in December 2002, our research agenda took a different course. We—the members of TERSG and contributors of this book—determined to investigate the research about teacher preparation (and literacy teacher preparation) of grades K–12 with the purpose of dispelling some of the common misconceptions about it. TERSG members wanted to bring the research record to bear on those "myths" (Berliner, 2000, p. 358) that somehow persist about teacher preparation, particularly in literacy. We began by brainstorming those so-called myths that, in some form or another, we all had confronted in our roles as literacy teacher educators.

To illustrate the kind of myths that persist about literacy teacher preparation, we began to tell one another our stories. Each of us had anecdotes about the public's misconceptions about literacy teacher preparation, the education sector, and policymakers. In one instance, a teacher educator teaching a literacy methods course asked teacher candidates to learn about literature circles (Daniels, 1994, 2002) as an instructional strategy for teaching literature in the middle-elementary grades. When one teacher candidate discussed this strategy with her cooperating teacher, the candidate was told, "Oh, forget all that! It's just one of those things they try to teach you at the university that are idealistic. These things never work in a real class!"

How, we all asked ourselves, do we counter such attitudes? Research on literature circles, for example, began in a real classroom. The strategy is used widely in real classrooms across the United States. Published research on literature circles (e.g., Daniels, 1994, 2002; Eeds & Wells, 1989; Flood, 1994; Grisham, 2001; Kauffman, Short, Crawford, Kahn, & Kaser, 1996) certainly refutes the notion that it is something that originated at the university level and is too "idealistic" to be implemented in various diverse classroom settings. "That's a myth!" we all cried.

In the course of our discussions, we decided to focus on the positive aspects of literacy teacher preparation. We compiled a list of 10 widely held understandings—rather than misunderstandings—about teacher preparation. After a great deal of discussion, we decided to examine closely the research base to document what we decided to call the "truths" about literacy teacher preparation, using the research base to support each truth.

Some of the TERSG members disliked the word *truth* because it sounded too absolute. However, most of us subscribe to a theoretical stance known as social constructivism. Based on the work of Vygotsky (1934/1962, 1934/1978) and others, Fosnot (1996) expresses this stance quite well:

> Constructivism is a theory about knowledge and learning; it describes both what "knowing" is and how one "comes to know." Based on work in psychology, philosophy, and anthropology, the theory describes knowledge as temporary, developmental, nonobjective, internally constructed, and socially and culturally mediated. Learning from this perspective is viewed as a self-regulatory process of struggling with the conflict between existing personal models of the world and discrepant new insights, constructing new representations and models of reality as a human meaning-making venture with culturally developed tools and symbols, and further negotiating such meaning though cooperative social activity, discourse, and debate. (p. ix)

Thus, when we use the word *truth*, we mean what has been established by the weight of research-based evidence in our field. Although all of us had been researching our own teaching practices over time, none of us really knew the full extent of the research base. It was as we began our yearlong effort to locate and read research bearing upon our particular truths that we began to realize the depth and breadth of the knowledge base in literacy teacher preparation. The truths we identified evolved as we read more research, and therefore the truths we present in this book are provisional truths, subject to change over time as new practices and new research evidence emerges. Despite this caveat, the truths that appear in this book are based upon the best existing evidence we have been able to locate. We must be honest in stating that there may be research that we have missed, although our search has been both wide and diligent. It also is incumbent upon us to be honest—we desire to frame our work in a positive way, and that is how each of us has surveyed the literature.

At this point, it seems germane to mention that the research base for teacher preparation has a fairly short history, with most research occurring since the 1950s. Most of the research that we read does not consist of large-scale field trials that lend themselves to cause-and-effect generalizations (Cochran-Smith, 2004). Many of the studies are self-studies by one or two teacher educators investigating their own practices. Some of the studies are descriptive, many are qualitative, and there are published studies that do not meet standards of rigor for the research methods that were used.

We do not contest that the knowledge base is limited, fractionalized, and in many cases, not able to be generalized. Teacher preparation research, which the education community often dismisses as lacking rigor, is a frequent target of conservative methodologists. There is, according to Cochran-Smith (2002), a "widespread perception that educational research is low quality, constantly contested and incapable of producing knowledge that improves educational policy and practice" (p. 188). However, there is still much research on literacy teacher preparation that has power and persuasiveness. A recent example of such work is the longitudinal study Darling-Hammond, Holtzman, Gatlin, and Heilig (2005) conducted in Houston, Texas, USA, on Teach for America (TFA) and its impact on students' academic outcomes. Finally, we point out that the vast majority of research on literacy teacher preparation (and teacher preparation in general) has been at the elementary level. Policymakers currently are directing more research and reform emphasis—including additional funding for research—toward secondary education, particularly in literacy.

Purpose and Organization of This Book

The purpose of this book is to make visible the efforts of literacy teacher educators to investigate and improve their own practices over time and bring to a wide audience the results of those efforts. We hope that our book will provide a broader focus on literacy teacher preparation and will be useful to teachers, teacher educators, literacy researchers, and policymakers. Our intent is to share our perspective—informed by research—with as many constituencies as possible.

After our initial research and discussion, we agreed on the following 10 truths, each of which forms a chapter of this book. Each chapter is organized similarly, beginning with an explanation of the particular truth being addressed. To aid the reader, we provide an overview of the chapter, including important points to remember. Next, each chapter contains a vignette (pseudonyms are used throughout the vignettes) that helps to personalize the topic for the reader and illustrate a real-world scenario. The balance of each chapter contains the information that we have compiled to support the truth.

Truth 1: Literacy teacher preparation is based on research. Janet R. Young and Roni Jo Draper address the topic of the knowledge base in literacy teacher preparation. They discuss the rigor, abundance, and quality of teacher preparation research in literacy; they also trace the more recent differences in what teacher educators are being asked to assess as the outcomes of literacy teacher preparation.

Truth 2: Teacher candidates meet increasingly demanding criteria for admissions and certification. Linda S. Wold discusses the improvement of standards-based teacher preparation programs in general over the past two decades and establishes the importance of teacher preparation in creating quality teachers. Wold outlines important changes in admissions criteria for teacher preparation programs and explains that the pool of teacher candidates is made up of increasingly higher numbers of promising students. Wold emphasizes that literacy education, situated within the general teacher preparation program, has benefited from the increased admissions criteria for teacher preparation programs, and, through literacy research, literacy education, in turn, has contributed to the improvement of teacher preparation.

Truth 3: Rigor in literacy course work emphasizes the integration of theory and practice. Carol D. Wickstrom, Leslie Patterson, and Cathy K. Zeek provide research evidence about rigor in teacher preparation programs. The authors argue that qualified teachers learn to become more expert through deliberate practice in and integration of content knowledge and pedagogy—in an arena that is amazingly complex.

Truth 4: Teacher preparation programs make a difference in teacher candidates' perspectives about literacy teaching. Karen E. Smith and Carole S. Rhodes investigate what it takes to become a teacher, making transparent how important teacher preparation programs are to the development of teacher candidates' views of themselves as literacy role models and identifying the many components of a literacy methods course focused on preparing quality literacy teachers.

Truth 5: Teacher preparation programs offer targeted field experiences in literacy. Susan Davis Lenski and Susan L. Nierstheimer carefully document the role of university course work and field experiences on teacher candidates' developing conceptions of teaching practices. The authors demonstrate how course work and field experiences interact to integrate theory and practice, producing novice teachers who are knowledgeable about content, conversant with pedagogy, and confident in their teaching practices.

Truth 6: Teacher preparation programs link literacy teaching with the demands of teaching in schools. Debra K. Wellman and Linda S. Wold investigate and detail the efforts of literacy teacher educators over the past 50 years to establish relevance in literacy teacher preparation through field experiences, teacher–educator reciprocal experiences in schools, and school–university collaborations such as Professional Development Schools (PDS).

Truth 7: Teacher preparation programs situate school curricula in the larger context of teaching and learning. Marva Cappello and Nancy Farnan examine the research on literacy teacher preparation curricula. They argue that specific school curricula are rightly situated within a continuum of types of literacy programs. In literacy methods courses, teacher candidates not only become familiar with basal programs and other materials currently in use, but they also learn the skills needed to judge the value of new programs to be adopted by their school districts. Literacy teacher preparation also focuses on principles to help new teachers learn to teach for meaning and transfer.

Truth 8: Traditional teacher preparation programs better prepare future literacy teachers than do alternative routes. Bette S. Bergeron traces the origin and myths surrounding the many alternative route (AR) programs currently in vogue. Next, she examines the research base that reflects that teacher candidates who are prepared traditionally in professional teacher preparation programs appear superior to those prepared in AR programs on a number of important criteria, including the integration of theory and practice, teacher retention, and K–12 student achievement in literacy.

Truth 9: Assessment has a dual purpose in teacher preparation programs. Thomas P. Crumpler and Ellen Spycher look at the way literacy teacher candidates are assessed in their credential programs for evidence of growth in their knowledge of teaching. The authors argue that no single assessment is sufficient for measuring the complexity of teaching, particularly in literacy. They lead readers through the existing research on assessment for admission to teacher preparation programs, licensing and certification, performance and professional growth, and teacher knowledge and quality of practice.

Truth 10: Teacher preparation programs graduate highly qualified novice teachers. Nancy Farnan and Dana L. Grisham argue that newly graduated literacy teachers are novices who need additional support and professional growth in their first years of teaching. They clarify what is meant by "highly qualified novices." They identify the strengths teacher preparation programs confer upon new teachers and identify areas of weakness that novices must convert into genuine areas of expertise during their first years of teaching. The authors argue that well-prepared novice teachers are in the first stages of a continuum of professional development.

The chapters are followed by a conclusion and an appendix. An appendix provides the reader with sources and resources that also support the truths.

Conclusion

It has been both hard work and a joy to put this volume together. The editors and authors all are literacy teacher educators, some in elementary education and some in secondary education. All of us have worked in education for many years and in diverse capacities, and each one of us began his or her career in public education. Together we have more years than we care to count of public school teaching experience. At some point in our teaching careers, all of us returned to school for advanced degrees in education because we believe in democratic public education and wanted to know more about it. We all became literacy teacher educators so we could make a positive difference and more widely contribute to the education of children. We have spent the rest of our professional lives in literacy teacher preparation. We are united in believing that this is an important volume because it takes a measured evidential stance toward teacher preparation, not an ideological one. We all work hard to do the best we can for our teacher candidates and for the students they teach. We do not think teacher preparation is perfect. We do know, however, that education is a profession that aims for continual self-improvement.

Acknowledgments

We would like to thank the TERSG members for their inspiration, ideas, and support. We also would like to thank our family members and friends, who have encouraged us to continue to learn how to become better teacher educators. Among those to whom we are indebted are Fran Lenski, Marc Grisham, and Rick Wold, the most supportive husbands in the world.

REFERENCES

Berliner, D.C. (2000). A personal response to those who bash teacher education. *Journal of Teacher Education, 51*(5), 358–371.

Berliner, D.C., Bell, J., & Biddle, B.J. (1996). *Manufactured crisis: Myths, fraud, and the attack on America's public schools.* Cambridge, MA: Perseus.

Bruce, B.C. (2002). Diversity and critical social engagement: How changing technologies enable new modes of literacy in changing circumstances. In D.E. Alvermann (Ed.), *Adolescents and literacies in a digital world* (pp. 1–18). New York: Peter Lang.

Cochran-Smith, M. (2002). What difference a definition makes: Highly qualified teachers, scientific research, and teacher education. *Journal of Teacher Education, 53*(3), 187–189.

Cochran-Smith, M. (2004). Ask a different question, get a different answer: The research base for teacher education. *Journal of Teacher Education, 55*(1), 111–115.

Daniels, H. (1994). *Literature response circles: Voice and choice in the student-centered classroom.* York, ME: Stenhouse.

Daniels, H. (2002). *Literature circles: Voice and choice in book clubs and reading groups* (2nd ed.). Portland, ME: Stenhouse.

Darling-Hammond, L., Holtzman, D.J., Gatlin, S.J., & Heilig, J.V. (2005, April). *Does teacher preparation matter? Evidence about teacher certification, Teach for America, and teacher effectiveness.* Paper presented at the American Educational Research Association, Montreal, Canada.

Eeds, M., & Wells, D. (1989). Grand conversations: An exploration of meaning construction in literature study groups. *Research in the Teaching of English, 23*(1), 4–29.

Flood, J. (1994). *Teacher book clubs: A study of teachers' and student teachers' participation in contemporary multicultural fiction literature discussion groups* (Reading Research Project No. 22). Athens, GA: National Reading Research Center.

Fosnot, C.T. (Ed.). (1996). *Constructivism: Theory, perspectives, and practices.* New York: Teachers College Press.

Grisham, D.L. (2001). Developing preservice teachers' perspectives on reader response. *Reading Horizons, 41*(4), 211–238.

Kauffman, G., Short, K.G., Crawford, K.M., Kahn, L., & Kaser, S. (1996). Examining the roles of teachers and students in literature circles across classroom contexts. In D.J. Leu, C.K. Kinzer, & K.A. Hinchman (Eds.), *Literacies for the 21st century: Research and practice* (45th yearbook of the National Reading Conference, pp. 373–384). Chicago: National Reading Conference.

Vygotsky, L.S. (1962). *Thought and language* (E. Hanfmann & G. Vakar, Eds. & Trans.). Cambridge, MA: MIT Press. (Original work published 1934)

Vygotsky, L.S. (1978). *Mind in society: The development of higher psychological processes* (M. Cole, V. John-Steiner, S. Scribner, & E. Souberman, Eds. & Trans.). Cambridge, MA: Harvard University Press. (Original work published 1934)

CONTRIBUTORS

Bette S. Bergeron
Professor and Head of Education
Arizona State University
    Polytechnic
Mesa, Arizona, USA

Marva Cappello
Assistant Professor of Teacher
    Education
San Diego State University
San Diego, California, USA

Thomas P. Crumpler
Associate Professor of Reading
    and Literacy
Illinois State University
Normal, Illinois, USA

Roni Jo Draper
Associate Professor of Content-
    Area Literacy
Brigham Young University
Provo, Utah, USA

Nancy Farnan
Director, School of Teacher
    Education
San Diego State University
San Diego, California, USA

Dana L. Grisham
Professor of Literacy Education
San Diego State University
San Diego, California, USA
and
Codirector, Center for the
    Advancement of Reading
California State University Office
    of the Chancellor
Sacramento, California, USA

Susan Davis Lenski
Professor of Literacy
Portland State University
Portland, Oregon, USA

Susan L. Nierstheimer
Assistant Professor of Literacy
    and Language
Purdue University
West Lafayette, Indiana, USA

Leslie Patterson
Professor of Reading
University of North Texas
Denton, Texas, USA

Carole S. Rhodes
Professor and Director of Education
    Research and Development
Queens College, City University
    of New York
Flushing, New York, USA

Karen E. Smith
Assistant Professor of Language
and Literacy
University of Manitoba
Winnipeg, Manitoba, Canada

Ellen Spycher
Assistant Professor of Curriculum
& Instruction
Illinois State University
Normal, Illinois, USA

Debra K. Wellman
Director of Student Teaching and
Assistant Professor of Reading
Rollins College
Winter Park, Florida, USA

Carol D. Wickstrom
Assistant Professor of Reading
University of North Texas
Denton, Texas, USA

Linda S. Wold
Assistant Professor of Literacy
Education
Loyola University Chicago
Chicago, Illinois, USA

Janet R. Young
Assisant Professor of Teacher
Education
Brigham Young University
Provo, Utah, USA

Cathy K. Zeek
Associate Professor and Chair,
Education Department
Lasell College
Newton, Massachusetts, USA

TRUTH 1

Literacy Teacher Preparation Is Based on Research

JANET R. YOUNG AND RONI JO DRAPER

◆ ◆ ◆

Literacy teacher educators are often faced with the competing demands of creating quality teacher preparation programs and conducting research on those programs. Thus, those charged with the privilege of preparing literacy teacher candidates for U.S. schools also are responsible for evaluating the effectiveness of their own teacher preparation programs and practices. By rigorously pursuing their research agendas, teacher educators may be brought to the point of having to be critical, not complimentary, about their own institutions or programs. These researchers commonly address issues found in other areas of teacher preparation research, including what counts as evidence of program effectiveness, how to examine the relation between teacher knowledge and student learning, and how to account for what teacher candidates bring to their preparation.

Within today's educational climate, the call for scientifically based research of the processes and products of literacy teacher preparation is pressing and sometimes strident. Because of heightened public awareness of the importance of literacy instruction in schools, pressure to openly examine the contributions of high-quality teacher preparation in ways acceptable to parents and policymakers often is acute. Literacy teacher educators employ a variety of methods that are similar to research in other fields to generate research evidence and build their knowledge base about preparing teachers to teach literacy in increasingly diverse classrooms.

Literacy teacher preparation is increasingly the focus of research. This focus has produced a growing body of research on literacy teacher preparation that relies on aspects of rigorous research, such as aligning the questions and design of the study, achieving valid and reliable data collection and analysis, and reaching reasonable conclusions based on verification. High-quality literacy teacher preparation programs are based on such research.

◆ ◆ ◆

Literacy Teacher Preparation: Ten Truths Teacher Educators Need to Know by Susan Davis Lenski, Dana L. Grisham, and Linda S. Wold, Editors. Copyright © 2006 by the International Reading Association.

CHAPTER HIGHLIGHTS

◆ Research on literacy teacher preparation presents challenges such as diversity in research perspectives and questions to be addressed, a broad range of contexts for literacy teacher preparation research, and considerable complexity in issues and practices to be studied.

◆ Literacy researchers appropriately select research methodologies based on their purposes, the questions they target, and the best ways to answer those questions.

◆ Decisions about literacy teacher preparation must continue to be based on research.

RESEARCH ON LITERACY TEACHER PREPARATION

Brittany, the literacy coordinator in an undergraduate teacher preparation program, calls the regularly scheduled meeting of the literacy faculty to order. After a few brief announcements, the group turns its attention to the primary agenda item for the day: refining one of the core assignments used during the past semester by several instructors across multiple sections of the same literacy methods course. Two of the literacy faculty members, Susan and John, begin a lively discussion about several aspects of the assignment that they think need to be changed based on their recent experiences in implementing the assessment assignment with their own classes. Several other literacy faculty members express their opinions on the proposed changes, then Lori, another literacy faculty member, suggests consulting the International Reading Association professional standards (2003) for guidance on what teacher candidates should know and be able to do upon completion of their teacher preparation programs. Her suggestion serves as a segue for Brittany to share the findings of a study about literacy teacher preparation and literacy assessment that she has recently located in a professional journal. As the conversation continues, the literacy faculty members draw from their own experiences, professional standards, and research on literacy teacher preparation to shape their revision of the literacy methods course assignment.

Although researchers have studied teacher preparation rather extensively for many years, interest in examining literacy teacher preparation is far more recent. A thorough search of literacy research, or even a cursory examination of the contents of the three volumes of the *Handbook of Reading Research* (Barr, Kamil, Mosenthal, & Pearson, 1991; Kamil, Mosenthal, Pearson, & Barr, 2000; Pearson, Barr, Kamil, & Mosenthal, 1984), reveals that in the past decade, literacy research in teacher preparation has increasingly become a primary focus for researchers (Anders, Hoffman, & Duffy, 2000).

In general, studies of literacy-related aspects of teacher preparation programs have been conducted on a relatively small scale, often undertaken by researchers within individual teacher preparation institutions. Such studies often focus on the overall effectiveness of teacher preparation programs in preparing teacher candidates as literacy teachers (e.g., Fang & Ashley, 2004) or on specific aspects of literacy teacher preparation programs such as reflection and inquiry (e.g., Quiocho & Ulanoff, 2004), autobiography (e.g., Bean, 1994; Wolf, Ballentine, & Hill, 2000), or technology in literacy programs (e.g., Hughes, Packard, & Pearson, 2000). Cross-institutional studies of literacy teacher preparation, which are studies simultaneously conducted at multiple sites, also are focused on either the general effectiveness of teacher preparation programs or on specific elements of literacy teacher preparation (e.g., Rosemary, Freppon, & Kinnucan-Welsch, 2002). These studies also have contributed to the growing knowledge base about effective preparation of literacy teachers.

Large-scale, multiple-site research studies on literacy teacher preparation are far rarer than small-scale, single-program studies, perhaps for good reasons. Funding for such large-scale research is difficult for researchers to obtain (Burkhardt & Shoenfeld, 2003; Cochran-Smith, 2004a). Clear agreement on questions that need to be addressed through large-scale research may be difficult for teacher educators, policymakers, or other stakeholders to reach because the purposes for research on literacy teacher preparation vary. For example, teacher educators who want to know about beginning teachers' satisfaction or teachers' literacy-related knowledge bases as they enter the teaching force pose different kinds of research questions than those whose evaluation of literacy teacher preparation program effectiveness is focused on teacher behaviors during their first year of teaching or on student achievement. In a similar manner, literacy teacher educators grounded in diverse research perspectives are likely to address diverse research questions and employ dissimilar research methodologies, which make large-scale studies more challenging (Hoffman & Pearson, 2000).

Further, the complex, contextualized nature of the task of preparing excellent literacy teachers makes large-scale research very difficult to conduct. Teacher preparation in higher education may include undergraduate, or four-year, certification programs, or five-year, postbaccalaureate or graduate programs. Also, teacher preparation programs can be found in both private- and state-sponsored public universities or colleges, and the programs vary significantly in size and student diversity. In each of these contexts, there are both universal and unique features that must be accounted for in large-scale research design, which makes such studies less common. Even among teacher preparation programs clearly aligned with professional standards, there is considerable diversity in policies and practices for preparing excellent literacy teachers (Hoffman, Roller, & The National Commission on Excellence in Elementary Teacher Preparation for Reading Instruction, 2001).

To make matters more difficult, large-scale research focused on the long-term effectiveness of literacy teacher preparation requires researchers to follow novice teachers into their first years of teaching, which may require tracking them into various locations that each present researchers with distinctive social, cultural, and political settings. Finally, the complex nature of literacy instruction across grade levels in such diverse settings defies "one-size-fits-all" instructional practices (e.g., literacy programs, materials, intervention strategies) that facilitate large-scale studies, particularly those with an experimental design.

In spite of the messiness of their endeavor, teacher educators should carefully examine the impact and quality of teacher preparation programs in literacy education. There is a need for research that explores not only the effects of literacy teacher preparation programs during teacher candidates' participation in them but also changes not immediately evident in those candidates. This need requires researchers to track program graduates into their beginning years as teachers, to examine program effects on the teachers themselves, and ultimately, to examine the impact of teacher preparation on student literacy learning. These are only some of the challenging expectations that frame methodological considerations for the current research agenda in literacy teacher preparation.

Methodological Considerations of Research on Literacy Teacher Preparation

Simply stated, research is an attempt to understand something through systematic data collection and analysis. As previously stated, the effectiveness of a given research study has to do with the care the researcher takes in aligning the questions and design of the study, achieving valid and reliable data collection and analysis, and reaching reasonable conclusions or making recommendations based on verification of research evidence. Although this list may seem fairly straightforward, it is not meant to suggest that meeting the challenges of rigor is simple or easy.

Often policymakers or others outside the education community erroneously equate rigor in educational research with experimental research design (Cochran-Smith, 2002b). However, rigor has less to do with any particular research design (e.g., experimental, ethnographic, case study, or longitudinal) and more to do with the care the researcher takes in planning and carrying out his or her research. One way researchers can conduct research is in the form of experiments in which participants are randomly assigned to groups and one group receives a treatment while another group (the control group) receives no treatment, and the participants of these groups are compared on some kind of outcome measure. This type of research is desirable because it attempts to answers questions such as "What works best?" Experimental and quasi-experimental research designs are employed appropriately when the purpose of the study is to compare treatment conditions, identify causal relationships among variables, or generalize the research findings within the context of similar situations or settings.

However, other forms of research designed to achieve different purposes can be equally valuable and rigorous. For example, researchers may want to determine how in-school mentors support novice teachers during practice teaching experiences (e.g., practica, field experiences, or student teaching). They may want to compare the decision-making processes of novice teachers with the decision-making processes of experienced teachers or examine the goals and objectives of various courses that teacher candidates take during their teacher preparation programs to determine whether they are receiving consistent information. An experimental design is not well suited to provide the rich explanatory evidence required for these descriptive studies; however, all of these questions could be answered with other research designs such as ethnography, case study, or content analysis.

Research Questions and Design Compatibility

As in other types of educational research, research on literacy teacher preparation asks important questions and employs appropriate methodologies for answering those questions. Experimental research is useful in determining cause-and-effect relationships; however, that research often can take place only when the researcher has created a sufficient foundational research base (Pearson, 2001). Therefore, research questions often progress through a research agenda that begins with foundational theory building and progresses to research that asks questions such as "What literacy teacher preparation programs have the greatest impact on student achievement in literacy and writing?" Indeed, this question is important and requires experimental research methodologies to answer it with any degree of confidence. However, before researchers can even ask questions such as these, they need to answer other foundational questions such as "What is the current state of literacy teacher preparation across the United States? What is the literacy knowledge base of teachers who exit teacher preparation programs? What characteristics of literacy teachers or features of literacy instruction have the greatest impact on student achievement in reading and writing?"

The National Commission on Excellence in Elementary Teacher Preparation for Reading Instruction, convened and funded by the International Reading Association (IRA), has begun to consider some of the foundational issues related to the preparation of literacy teachers. For example, members of the multisite commission have published research articles that describe the features of literacy teacher preparation programs identified as excellent (Harmon et al., 2001; Hoffman et al., 2001), the beliefs and knowledge base about literacy instruction of beginning teachers who have graduated from programs identified as excellent (Flint et al., 2001; Maloch et al., 2003), and the changes made to a literacy teacher preparation program as the university faculty members participated in the Commission's activities (Keehn et al., 2003). These research studies serve to build a theoretical knowledge base of literacy teacher preparation that addresses the question asked by Pearson (2001), "What does reading teacher education look like?" (p. 18).

However, quality research consists of more than just asking questions; it requires research methodologies specifically designed to answer those questions. In the studies we already mentioned, researchers primarily used qualitative research design methodologies. These methodologies allowed the researchers to seek opinions of faculty members and recent graduates from varying sizes and types of literacy teacher preparation programs, to gather narrative descriptions of the programs and beginning teacher practices, and to create descriptions of teachers' practices based on classroom observations. In fact, rigorous qualitative research designs rely on multiple data sources to corroborate results. For example, Keehn and colleagues (2003) reported the changes to the undergraduate literacy teacher preparation programs as they participated in the Commission's activities. Rather than rely wholly on self-reported data from literacy teacher educators, the researchers analyzed program documents such as syllabi and program descriptions before and after participating in the Commission's activities. Furthermore, they reported limitations to their study, pointing out that the study did not include observations of literacy methods courses that would have affected their results.

Data Management

For research to be considered rigorous, researchers must carefully collect and analyze data. Indeed, collecting data is frequently the easiest part of a research study. However, careful data analysis, whether it is qualitative or quantitative, requires researchers to make decisions before, during, and after analysis, and to base those decisions on sound understandings of how to conduct research. For example, the study conducted by Maloch and colleagues (2003) required conducting telephone interviews with novice teachers at various sites three times over an academic year. Because the open-ended interviews were conducted by different individuals that resulted in interviews of various lengths, the researchers carefully analyzed the interview data for consistency. Once the researchers were confident that the interviews were consistent across sites and times, they analyzed the entire data set inductively over four separate rounds of analysis. These rounds of analysis allowed multiple researchers at multiple sites to identify themes and patterns by looking for disconfirming evidence and to check the entire data set to see that the study's overall findings were representative across all sites.

Researchers who use other methodologies must demonstrate care in data collection and analysis as they do in cross-institutional research. In a nested design, or a study of a study, Broaddus (2000) conducted a case study of a case study. She studied a teacher candidate who, as part of her literacy teacher preparation program, conducted case-study research of an emergent reader. At both levels of inquiry, Broaddus and the teacher candidate attended to conventions of qualitative data management, including prolonged engagement with and persistent observation of the research participant, peer debriefing, self-as-instrument examination (a careful description of how the researcher made sense of the data), and triangulation of data sources (collection of data from more than one data source to corroborate and strengthen the trustworthiness of the findings). Such care in managing and analyzing data is a hallmark of rigor in a broad range of research designs.

Reasonable Research Conclusions

Reasonable research conclusions have to do with the care researchers take in generalizing results across appropriate populations. When researchers design studies that seek to cast a wide net, gathering data from many individuals in a variety of locations or circumstances, they increase their power to generalize their findings to broad populations. The cost of such an approach, however, is the ability to examine in open-ended ways the phenomenon they are studying. For example, in one of the initial studies conducted by the Commission (Hoffman et al., 2001), researchers used survey data from 949 teacher educators who were members of IRA to characterize current practices in literacy teacher preparation in the United States. The large data set, which represented a 60% response rate among potential respondents, allowed the researchers to draw conclusions about current teacher preparation practices with a rather high level of confidence. Even so, the researchers were careful to acknowledge the study's sample bias toward literacy teacher educators who were members of IRA. They also rightly noted that the large scale of the study dictated closed responses for most of questions on the survey. Respondents were, therefore, limited in the depth and diversity of their responses, so researchers had to carefully generalize their findings.

Nonexperimental research, often conducted on a much smaller scale than the large-scale study, has been recognized by literacy teacher educators as a rich source of knowledge about literacy teacher preparation (Anders et al., 2000; National Institute of Child Health and Human Development [NICHD], 2000; Pearson, 2001). Such research is particularly useful for researchers identifying themes and formulating further research questions. It is important to remember that it is neither the intent nor the purpose of researchers conducting individual studies of this sort to generalize the results to all situations. Rather, findings of such studies, when examined collectively, assume the character of individual tiles in a mosaic. Patterns across studies emerge; findings of one study may be interpreted in light of findings in prior research. Carefully conducted reviews of the literature (e.g., Anders et al., 2000; Hoffman & Pearson, 2000; NICHD, 2000; Snow, Burns, & Griffin, 1998) allow the findings from a broad range of studies to converge, which creates a knowledge base to help literacy teacher educators draw reasonable conclusions about the preparation of literacy teachers. Well-crafted reviews also allow literacy teacher educators to identify trends in the evidence as well as gaps in the literacy teacher preparation research.

In addition to increasing the breadth of studies or considering cumulative findings of many studies, reasonableness of conclusions from research is enhanced when researchers are careful that their conclusions do not reach beyond the scope of the design of the study, but rather are thoroughly grounded in their data and analysis. Carefully conducted longitudinal research provides one avenue for ensuring this aspect of rigor because researchers are afforded the opportunity to examine their preliminary findings based on evidence that accumulates over time. By following elementary-grade literacy teachers and secondary-grade language arts teachers into their first three years of teaching, Grossman and colleagues (2000) noted that concepts and practices emphasized by literacy teacher educators during teacher preparation were more evident during novice teachers' second year of teaching rather than their first year of teaching. The ability to check the constancy of their initial conclusions over time was made possible through rigorously conducted longitudinal research.

Conclusion

The claim that literacy teacher preparation is based on research is not meant in any way to suggest that literacy teacher educators and literacy researchers have enough information about the preparation of literacy teachers. There is much we still need to know, such as "How can literacy teacher educators optimize the preservice experiences of literacy teacher candidates so that they are prepared to effectively teach students who have diverse needs?" This is a time of "incredible impatience in the policy world" (Pearson, 2001, p. 5) for research that advances our knowledge about effective literacy teacher preparation. Literacy teacher educators caught between the pressure for standards-based reform in literacy teacher preparation and the pressure to prepare teachers with a "sense of mission that allows them to maintain an independent stance in the face of the pressures to conform and comply" (Duffy, 2002, p. 339) need to be able to make decisions about literacy teacher preparation based on empirical evidence, rather than professional judgment (Cochran-Smith, 2004b; Pearson, 2001).

However, there may be questions that research cannot answer—questions about ideals, values, and beliefs about literacy teaching and learning (Cochran-Smith, 2002a). The challenge for literacy teacher educators is to continue to keep decisions about their literacy teacher preparation programs grounded in research while understanding the limitations of that research. Furthermore, literacy teacher educators must help policymakers and other stakeholders interested in the preparation of teachers understand the potential and the limitations of research in general and specifically of literacy teacher preparation research. Literacy teacher educators must not allow discussion and debate about literacy teacher preparation to become void of talk about the purpose of literacy education, the value of literacy education, or the role of literacy in preparing students for participation in a democratic society.

REFERENCES

Anders, P.L., Hoffman, J.V., & Duffy, G.G. (2000). Teaching teachers to teach reading: Paradigm shifts, persistent problems, and challenges. In M.L. Kamil, P.B. Mosenthal, P.D. Pearson, & R. Barr (Eds.), *Handbook of reading research* (Vol. 3, pp. 719–742). Mahwah, NJ: Erlbaum.

Barr, R., Kamil, M.L., Mosenthal, P., & Pearson, P.D. (Eds.). (1991). *Handbook of reading research* (Vol. 2). White Plains, NY: Longman.

Bean, T.W. (1994). A constructivist view of preservice teachers' attitudes toward reading through case study analysis of autobiographies. In C.K. Kinzer & D.J. Leu (Eds.), *Multidimensional aspects of literacy research, theory, and practice* (43rd yearbook of the National Reading Conference, pp. 370–379). Chicago: National Reading Conference.

Broaddus, K. (2000). From peacemaker to advocate: A preservice teacher's case study of an emergent reader. *Journal of Literacy Research, 32*(4), 571–597.

Burkhardt, H., & Schoenfeld, A.H. (2003). Improving educational research: Toward a more useful, more influential, and better-funded enterprise. *Educational Researcher, 32*(9), 3–14.

Cochran-Smith, M. (2002a). The research base for teacher education: Metaphors we live (and die) by. *Journal of Teacher Education, 53*(4), 283–285.

Cochran-Smith, M. (2002b). What a difference a definition makes: Highly qualified teachers, scientific research, and teacher education. *Journal of Teacher Education, 53*(3), 187–189.

Cochran-Smith, M. (2004a). Ask a different question, get a different answer: The research base for teacher education. *Journal of Teacher Education, 55*(2), 111–115.

Cochran-Smith, M. (2004b). Taking stock in 2004: Teacher education in dangerous times. *Journal of Teacher Education, 55*(1), 3–7.

Duffy, G.G. (2002). Visioning and the development of outstanding teachers. *Reading Research and Instruction, 41*(4), 331–344.

Fang, Z., & Ashley, C. (2004). Preservice teachers' interpretations of a field-based reading block. *Journal of Teacher Education, 55*(1), 39–54.

Flint, A.S., Leland, C.H., Patterson, B., Hoffman, J.V., Sailors, M.W., Mast, M.A., et al. (2001). "I'm still figuring out how to do this teaching thing": A cross-site analysis of reading preparation programs on beginning teachers' instructional practices and decisions. In C.M. Roller (Ed.), *Learning to teach reading: Setting the research agenda* (pp. 100–118). Newark, DE: International Reading Association.

Grossman, P.L., Valencia, S.W., Evans, K., Thompson, C., Martin, S., & Place, N. (2000). *Transitions into teaching: Learning to teach writing in teacher education.* New York: National Research Center on English Learning and Achievement.

Harmon, J., Hedrick, W., Martinez, M., Perez, B., Keehn, S., Fine, J.C., et al. (2001). Features of excellence of reading teacher preparation programs. In J.V. Hoffman, D.L. Schallert, C.M. Fairbanks, J. Worthy, & B. Maloch (Eds.), *Fiftieth yearbook of the National Reading Conference* (pp. 262–274). Chicago: National Reading Conference.

Hoffman, J., & Pearson, P.D. (2000). Reading teacher education in the next millennium: What your grandmother's teacher didn't know that your granddaughter's teacher should. *Reading Research Quarterly, 35*, 28–44.

Hoffman, J., Roller, C.M., & The National Commission on Excellence in Elementary Teacher Preparation for Reading Instruction. (2001). The IRA Excellence in Reading Teacher Preparation Commission's report: Current practices in reading teacher education at the undergraduate level in the United States. In C.M. Roller (Ed.), *Learning to teach reading: Setting the research agenda* (pp. 32–79). Newark, DE: International Reading Association.

Hughes, J.E., Packard, B.W., & Pearson, P.D. (2000). Preservice teachers' perceptions of using hypermedia and video to examine the nature of literacy instruction. *Journal of Literacy Research, 32*(4), 599–629.

International Reading Association (IRA). (2003). *Standards for reading professionals—Revised 2003.* Newark, DE: Author.

Kamil, M.L., Mosenthal, P.B., Pearson, P.D., & Barr, R. (Eds.). (2000). *Handbook of reading research* (Vol. 3). Mahwah, NJ: Erlbaum.

Keehn, S., Martinez, M., Harmon, J., Hedrick, W., Steinmetz, L., & Perez, B. (2003). Teacher preparation in reading: A case study of change in one university-based undergraduate program. In C.M. Fairbanks, J. Worthy, B. Maloch, J.V. Hoffman, & D.L. Schallert (Eds.), *Fifty-second yearbook of the National Reading Conference* (pp. 230–244). Chicago: National Reading Conference.

Maloch, B., Flint, A.S., Eldridge, D., Harmon, J., Loven, R., Fine, J.C., et al. (2003). Understandings, beliefs, and reported decision making of first-year teachers from different reading teacher preparation programs. *The Elementary School Journal, 103*(5), 431–457.

National Institute of Child Health and Human Development (NICHD). (2000). *Report of the National Reading Panel. Teaching children to read: An evidence-based assessment of the scientific research literature on reading and its implications for reading instruction* (NIH Publication No. 00-4769). Washington, DC: U.S. Government Printing Office.

Pearson, P.D. (2001). Learning to teach reading: The status of the knowledge base. In C.M. Roller (Ed.), *Learning to teach reading: Setting the research agenda* (pp. 4–19). Newark, DE: International Reading Association.

Pearson, P.D., Barr, R., Kamil, M.L., & Mosenthal, P. (1984). *Handbook of reading research.* New York: Longman.

Quiocho, A.M.L., & Ulanoff, S.H. (2004). Developing inquiry questions: Encouraging reflective practice in a language and literacy methods course. *Action in Teacher Education, 25*(4), 1–8.

Rosemary, C.A., Freppon, P., & Kinnucan-Welsch, K. (with Grogan, P., Feist-Willis, J., Zimmerman, B., et al.). (2002). Improving literacy teaching through structured collaborative inquiry in classroom and university clinical settings. In D.L. Schallert, C.M. Fairbanks, J. Worthy, B. Maloch, & J.V. Hoffman (Eds.), *Fifty-first yearbook of the National Reading Conference* (pp. 368–382). Chicago: National Reading Conference.

Snow, C.E., Burns, M.S., & Griffin, P. (Eds.). (1998). *Preventing reading difficulties in young children.* Washington, DC: National Academy Press.

Wolf, S.A., Ballentine, D., & Hill, L.A. (2000). "Only connect!" Cross-cultural connections in the reading lives of preservice teachers and children. *Journal of Literacy Research, 32*(4), 533–569.

TRUTH 2

Teacher Candidates Meet Increasingly Demanding Criteria for Admissions and Certification

LINDA S. WOLD

❖ ❖ ❖

Teacher preparation is an area that has changed greatly over the past two decades. During that time, teacher preparation programs have established higher admission and exit requirements, revised and updated certification criteria, and enforced performance standards for teachers. Almost all teacher preparation programs now require entrance examinations for admissions and exit examinations for certification. Admission to teacher preparation programs across the United States also requires higher grade point averages than it did 20 years ago. According to Mitchell, the associate vice president for accreditation of the National Council for Accreditation of Teacher Education (A. Mitchell, personal communication, January 11, 2005), more than half of all teacher preparation programs now are nationally accredited and meet approved standards developed by the National Board for Professional Teaching Standards (2004) and the Interstate New Teacher Assessment and Support Consortium (1992). These standards provide a foundation for research-based best practice and guide instruction in ways that positively impact student learning. The intent of institutions of higher education in using these standards is to influence teacher certification and program guidelines to shape the quality of teacher preparation.

❖ ❖ ❖

Literacy Teacher Preparation: Ten Truths Teacher Educators Need to Know by Susan Davis Lenski, Dana L. Grisham, and Linda S. Wold, Editors. Copyright © 2006 by the International Reading Association.

A VIEW OF TEACHER PREPARATION IN LITERACY

A dozen university faculty members and administrative staff gather around clustered tables to negotiate the student grade point average (GPA) for entrance into an undergraduate elementary teacher preparation program after students' first two years of course work. An intense conversation ensues. Some faculty members ask, "Is it fair to require students entering the teacher preparation program to earn a 2.75 GPA rather than a 2.5?" Advocates for a so-called developmental program stance argue that students who may not seem prepared or who may not qualify for the program based on their GPAs could become outstanding teachers. Others argue that students must have strong intellectual skills to teach successfully, especially in literacy teaching. Following an hour-long debate, the meeting adjourns after participants approve the higher GPA requirement.

The faculty bases this important decision on the fact that those who become teachers need to perform well in the foundational educational courses that set the standard for quality future performance. Some faculty members endorse the decision by stating,

> We want our teacher candidates to know best practices and be able to apply important teaching and learning strategies effectively. We believe that students' first two years of college performance strongly reveal their capacity to become quality teachers. We have also observed that students with higher GPAs demonstrate stronger skills in literacy teaching.

C riteria for admission into U.S. teacher preparation programs, both at the elementary and the secondary level, have steadily increased in the past few decades. As one example of more demanding criteria, teacher preparation programs across the United States are raising the GPA required for entrance into teacher preparation programs, suggesting that higher education institutions are choosing to select more "intellectually able candidates" (Allen, 2003, p. 83). The opening vignette illustrates that teacher educators are generally committed to raising academic requirements to ensure a stronger pool of teacher candidates.

Profound changes in teacher preparation requirements have caused angst in some faculty departments. Because admission requirements may exclude minority candidates from the profession (Smith, Miller, & Joy, 1988), decisions are encouraged that uphold a dual purpose: Faculty honor the diversity of the candidates while simultaneously recruiting excellent prospective teachers.

Changes in teacher preparation programs' admissions criteria help to suggest that teachers are more qualified and knowledgeable, particularly in literacy education, than ever before. Darling-Hammond and Youngs (2002) found that increasingly rigorous criteria in teacher preparation have, in fact, produced more highly qualified, knowledgeable, and competent teachers. Darling-Hammond and Youngs report two findings that relate to teacher preparation that they gathered from a thorough review of research on teacher qualification and its impact on student achievement: Teacher certification is related to effective teaching, which impacts student achievement, and graduates of teacher preparation programs are strong academically and prepared for their jobs.

It makes sense that when research suggests that teacher candidates are better prepared to impact student achievement, an extension of this argument also is warranted for literacy education.

Kantor and Lowe (2004) attest that quality education for students means "a strong academic curriculum taught by engaged, engaging, and well-educated teachers" (p. 6), and one of the goals of the National Commission on Teaching and America's Future (1996) is to provide every student with what should be his or her educational birthright, including access to competent, caring, and qualified teaching (Darling-Hammond, 1997). Therefore, establishing the link between quality teachers' accomplishments and their students' success is critically important (Goldhaber & Anthony, 2004). It makes sense that student success will follow with sustained and committed support to better teaching and learning and documentation of implemented best-practice teaching (Teitel, 2000).

Although one can infer that better quality literacy teaching results in improved student achievement; research, however, has yet to definitively establish this link. According to the International Reading Association (IRA; 2003), no conclusive causal studies exist to verify the impact of teacher preparation on the academic outcomes of the literacy of K–12 students. Yet some researchers (Ferguson, 1998; Harste, 1977, 1978) have argued that the development of quality teachers matters greatly to student achievement, and there are studies that provide correlational evidence in this direction. For example, in his analysis of teachers' expertise in 900 Texas school districts, Ferguson (1991) found that the qualifications of teachers (i.e., their scores on licensing tests, advanced course work in graduate school, and teaching experience) were the single most important factor in students' literacy and mathematics achievement.

Research on Teacher Preparation Programs

In a comprehensive survey by the National Center for Education Information (NCEI), Feistritzer (1999) analyzed changes in U.S. teacher preparation programs by comparing data collected in 1983 to corresponding data collected in 1998. One third of all teacher preparation programs responded to the survey. Results indicated strong trends in the increase of admissions criteria for teacher preparation programs, demographic changes in teacher candidate populations, and specific adjustments in teacher preparation program requirements across the United States. The results of the NCEI survey and two studies sponsored by IRA (Hoffman, Roller, & The National Commission on Excellence in Elementary Teacher Preparation for Reading Instruction, 2001; IRA, 2003) provide the basis for the subsequent analyses of literacy teacher preparation programs (Maloch, Fine, & Flint, 2002/2003). Recent National Board for Professional Teaching Standards (NBPTS) studies (Goldhaber & Anthony, 2004; Goldhaber, Perry, & Anthony, 2003) also support the connection between increased teacher certification requirements and student achievement gains, although research is still needed to provide further causal evidence. The NBPTS expects to create similar standards to guide teacher candidates; these standards also should have an impact on literacy education.

Raising the Standards for Teacher Candidates

More stringent standards for teacher preparation programs at the undergraduate and graduate level include entrance, exit, and certification requirements and a professional standards focus. By initiating more consistent and rigorous standards in these areas, the bar has been raised for teacher candidates.

Requirements for Admission to Teacher Preparation Programs

As previously mentioned, teacher preparation has changed dramatically in the past two decades. Almost 100% of teacher preparation institutions in the United States now require candidates to pass an entrance examination for admission into their programs. In comparison, only 40% of teacher preparation programs required an entrance examination in 1983. Teacher candidates' GPAs have risen from 2.29 to 3.0 for at least one third of all teacher candidates in undergraduate programs. Some programs also require multiple criteria that include GPAs, test scores, portfolio assessments, and written essays. Exit criteria, which a majority of teacher preparation programs use, validate candidates' knowledge and skill in general and specific content areas (Feistritzer, 1999).

Certification also provides adherence to program requirements. The fact that a broad use of more rigorous standards validates teacher certification supports the premise that better prepared and more competent teachers will perform better in the classroom and will be able to increase student achievement results (National Center for Education Statistics, 1999). One half of all U.S. teacher certification programs are using the National Council for Accreditation of Teacher Education standards to demonstrate teacher competency in the preparation of teacher candidates (Darling-Hammond, 2001). These standards provide some quality assurance that teacher candidates are developing the knowledge and skills they need to be effective teachers.

Certification, among other measures, establishes a "minimum standard for responsible practice" (Darling-Hammond & Youngs, 2002, p. 16) and serves as a potent reminder that there is room to develop more effective teaching practices. In 1998, one third more teachers received certification than in 1983, which raised the number of certified teachers from 135,000 to 201,000. Forty-one percent of elementary and secondary teachers also have a master's degree in an area of specialization or content area, which indicates that teachers who are seeking advanced graduate degrees are gaining a stronger knowledge base for teaching in specific fields.

Professional Standards and Teacher Preparation Programs

The large-scale analysis of NBPTS-certified teachers in North Carolina is one direct measure of the widely presumed effect that more highly qualified teachers produce greater student achievement gains. These national board certified teachers, who taught with a professional standards focus, performed better than noncertified teachers on teacher certification examinations, and their teaching resulted in higher student gains in literacy and math (Goldhaber & Anthony, 2004). When analyzing the baseline data, NBPTS (2004) researchers found that higher teacher quality positively influenced the achievement of students who had poor literacy skills. These students' test results showed an increase in literacy scores, thereby helping close the achievement gap. The same relationship also is considered regarding teacher candidates, although there is still a need to develop a strong research base in the area of literacy teacher preparation (IRA, 2003).

Relation Among Teacher Preparation, Teacher Certification, and Student Performance

Controversy exists about the research regarding more stringent teacher preparation entrance requirements and certification. The Education Commission of the States (Allen, 2003) found only two studies that followed a stringent research protocol that explored the relation between academic success and teaching effectiveness. Darling-Hammond and Youngs (2002) argue that there is a positive relationship among institutional requirements and preparation of quality teachers. In addition, IRA (2003) also demonstrated a significant impact on student literacy outcomes when students were taught by excellent literacy teachers. It is clear that further large-scale studies can help to confirm the connection between the academic success of literacy teachers and student academic outcomes.

Conclusion

The profile of teacher candidates has changed significantly since the implementation of more stringent standards, higher admission requirements, and upgraded certification criteria. Literacy teacher preparation is situated within most teacher preparation programs and has benefited from the improvements in general teacher preparation programs. Researchers also have argued that research in teacher preparation and literacy education has served to continually improve the quality and features of teacher preparation programs (Darling-Hammond, 1997, 1998; Maloch, Fine, & Flint, 2002/2003; Maloch et al., 2003). Teacher preparation programs are continuing to develop into student-based programs and have improved over the past 20 years. Teacher educators continue to prepare teacher candidates who will be engaged in teaching multiple content areas while using research-based strategies to instruct their students. As these teachers walk into their first classrooms, they will be teaching a diverse group of students and will be called upon to provide instructional guidance for these students in an era of exploding knowledge bases. These are critical and complex challenges for quality teaching (Schwartz, 1996). Despite the challenges, the current evidence provided by accountability and licensure testing suggests that teacher preparation is positive, enduring, and "better today than at any time in the past" (Imig & Switzer, 1996, p. 223).

REFERENCES

Allen, M.B. (2003). *Eight questions on teacher preparation: What does the research say?* Denver, CO: Education Commission of the States.

Darling-Hammond, L. (1997). *Doing what matters most: Investing in quality teaching.* Sacramento: The California State University Institute for Education Reform.

Darling-Hammond, L. (1998, September). *How can we ensure a caring, competent, qualified teacher for every child? Strategies for solving the dilemmas of teacher supply, demand, and standards.* Paper presented at the meeting of the American Federation of Teachers/National Education Association, Washington, DC. Retrieved November 30, 2003, from http://www.middleweb.com/TchRcrtLDH.html

Darling-Hammond, L. (2001). Standard setting in teaching: Changes in licensing, certification, and assessment. In V. Richardson (Ed.), *Handbook of research on teaching* (4th ed., pp. 751–776). Washington, DC: American Educational Research Association.

Darling-Hammond, L., & Youngs, P. (2002). Defining "highly qualified teachers": What does "scientifically-based research" actually tell us? *Educational Researcher, 31*(9), 13–25.

Feistritzer, C.E. (1999). *The making of a teacher: A report on teacher preparation in the U.S.* Retrieved April 22, 2005, from http://www.edutopia.org/php/resources.php?id=item_216595

Ferguson, R.F. (1991). Paying for public education: New evidence on how and why money matters. *Harvard Journal of Legislation, 28,* 465–498.

Ferguson, R.F. (1998). Teachers' perceptions and expectations and the black–white test score gap. In C. Jencks & M. Phillips (Eds.), *The black–white test score gap* (pp. 273–317). Washington, DC: Brookings Institute Press.

Goldhaber, D., & Anthony, E. (2004). *Can teacher quality be effectively assessed?* Retrieved April 22, 2005, from http://www.urban.org/template.cfm?template=/taggedcontent/view publication.cfm&publicationid=8772&navmenuid=95

Goldhaber, D., Perry, D., & Anthony, E. (2003). *NBPTS certification: Who applies and what factors are associated with success?* Retrieved April 22, 2005, from http://www.urban.org/template.cfm?template=/taggedcontent/viewpublication.cfm&publicationid=8324&navme nuid=95

Harste, J.C. (1977). Understanding the hypothesis: It's the teacher that makes the difference, part I. *Reading Horizons, 18*(1), 32–43.

Harste, J.C. (1978). Understanding the hypothesis: It's the teacher that makes the difference, part II. *Reading Horizons, 18*(2), 89–98.

Hoffman, J.V., Roller, C.M., & The National Commission on Excellence in Elementary Teacher Preparation for Reading Instruction. (2001). The IRA Excellence in Reading Teacher Preparation Commission's report: Current practices in reading teacher education at the undergraduate level in the United States. In C.M. Roller (Ed.), *Learning to teach reading: Setting the research agenda* (pp. 32–79). Newark, DE: International Reading Association.

Imig, D.G., & Switzer, T.J. (1996). Changing teacher education programs. Restructuring collegiate-based teacher education. In J. Sikula, T.J. Buttery, & E. Guyton (Ed.), *Handbook of research on teacher education* (2nd ed., pp. 213–226). New York: Macmillan.

International Reading Association (IRA). (2003). *Executive summary of the National Commission on Excellence in Elementary Teacher Preparation for Reading Instruction.* Retrieved April 22, 2005, from http://www.reading.org/downloads/resources/1061teacher_ed_com_summary.pdf

Interstate New Teacher Assessment and Support Consortium. (1992). *Model standards for beginning teacher licensing and development: A resource for state dialogue* [Electronic version]. Washington, DC: Council of Chief State School Officers. Retrieved August 30, 2005, from http://www.ccsso.org/projects/interstate_new_teacher_assessment_and_support_consortium

Kantor, H., & Lowe, R. (2004). Reflections on history and quality education. *Educational Researcher, 33*(5), 6–10.

Maloch, B., Fine, J., & Flint, A.S. (2002/2003). "I just feel like I'm ready": Exploring the influence of quality teacher preparation on beginning teachers. *The Reading Teacher, 56,* 348–350.

Maloch, B., Flint, A.S., Eldridge, D., Harmon, J., Loven, R., Fine, J.C., et al. (2003). Understandings, beliefs, and reported decision making of first-year teachers from different reading teacher preparation programs. *The Elementary School Journal, 103*(5), 431–457.

National Board for Professional Teaching Standards (NBPTS). (2004). *National Board for Professional Teaching Standards Candidate Resource Center.* Retrieved May 17, 2003, from http://www.nbpts.org/candidates

National Center for Education Statistics. (1999). *Teacher quality: A report on the preparation and qualifications of public school teachers.* Retrieved February 8, 2002, from http://www.nces.ed.gov/pubs2002/digest2001/ch3.asp

National Commission on Teaching and America's Future. (1996). *What matters most: Teaching for America's future.* Retrieved April 28, 2005, from http://www.zuni.k12.nm.us/ias/21te/nwrel/what.htm

Schwartz, H. (1996). The changing nature of teacher education. In J. Sikula, T.J. Buttery, & E. Guyton (Eds.), *Handbook of research on teacher education* (2nd ed., pp. 3–13). New York: Macmillan.

Smith, G.P., Miller, M.C., & Joy, J. (1988). A case study of the impact of performance-based testing on the supply of minority teachers. *Journal of Teacher Education, 39*(4), 45–53.

Teitel, L. (with Abdal-Haqq, I.). (2000). *Assessing the impacts of professional development schools.* Washington, DC: American Association of Colleges for Teacher Education Publications.

Rigor in Literacy Course Work Emphasizes the Integration of Theory and Practice

CAROL D. WICKSTROM, LESLIE PATTERSON,
AND CATHY K. ZEEK

◆ ◆ ◆

Literacy course work is much more rigorous than teacher candidates often expect, but that rigor might be of a different nature than the rigor of courses in other disciplines. For example, teacher candidates often find that the application of ideas to practical teaching situations takes thought and creativity. Literacy course work is based on professional standards and goals that emphasize the use of integrated learning theory and human development with literacy and writing processes. The rigor of literacy course work also can include the evaluation of teaching experiences in K–12 classrooms.

Teacher candidates find that, although the content of literacy courses is not difficult to comprehend, they are expected to apply theory and practice in widely varied classroom settings. This type of problem solving goes beyond the memorization of facts to the application of ideas in real-world situations.

◆ ◆ ◆

A VIEW OF LITERACY COURSE WORK

Rigorous literacy methods courses cause teacher candidates to think in new ways. Many teacher candidates think that these courses will entail only creating bulletin boards, booklists, and conducting reading groups. One teacher candidate, Jacob, says that he finds literacy methods courses rigorous and much more difficult than he has anticipated:

> I remember when I took my first college course. It was in a big lecture hall, and I had to listen to the lecture, take notes, take two tests, and write one paper for the entire course. Throughout college, I became adept at taking multiple-choice tests and writing term papers. I thought I had learning all figured out.

Jacob excels in undergraduate courses that call for memorization and recall. When Jacob begins teacher certification courses, however, he faces a different kind of learning. In literacy teacher preparation courses, Jacob is faced with the complex application of theory and practice, which he finds challenging. After his first literacy methods course, Jacob says,

> I'm using my mind in creative, new ways in this course, and I'm finally finding out that college was the challenge I had expected it to be. This type of learning is what I want in my life and the lives of the students that I teach in the future.

Rigor is an ambiguous concept. In teacher preparation programs, rigor could mean that admission standards are high or that the programs attract high-achieving college students. Sometimes the term *rigor* implies that the work is difficult, high grades are difficult to obtain, or the content is challenging. Rigor also could mean that research and teaching methods are difficult for students to understand. However, none of these perceptions of rigor actually describes the learning that is accomplished in literacy methods course work. Rigor in literacy methods courses entails using knowledge from theory and practice to make effective instructional decisions.

Papson (1995) views rigor as a rhetorical device. He states that "rigor is a politically dangerous rhetoric because it has no alternative. Rigor is not debatable; only how it is measured" (p. 6). According to this definition, rigor needs to be defined within the context in which it will be used. In a literacy methods course, for example, a rigorous curriculum would require teacher candidates to develop a personal theory of literacy that is grounded on the theories presented in the course work and to use that personal theory to develop teaching lessons. Teacher candidates also need to make judgments about the practical aspects of literacy theory, determining which ideas to use in their repertoire of teaching strategies. During field experiences, then, teacher candidates experiment with some of their ideas, reflect on their successes and problems, and make adjustments to their belief structure. This process applies theories in ways that can be considered rigorous, according to the context of teacher preparation.

In most U.S. colleges and universities, especially in the wake of reforms over the last 20 years, teacher preparation programs have increased in rigor. For example, the Texas teacher preparation curriculum requires every teacher candidate to major in a single content area for high school teaching or in "interdisciplinary studies"—a composite of the core content subjects— for elementary school teaching. Each teacher candidate must pass two statewide exit tests, one in pedagogy and one in the content area related to the candidate's teaching field, which is often literacy. Overall grade point average (GPA) requirements to enter teacher preparation programs in Texas generally are 3.0 or higher. These examples of a state's expectations of teacher candidates illustrate the ways teacher preparation programs have increased the accountability of their graduates. Teacher candidates, therefore, must show their knowledge of pedagogy in general, and many teacher candidates choose literacy as their content subject. The GPAs and test scores of teacher candidates indicate the rigor of the literacy program. Most states have similar criteria for teacher candidates.

Standards for rigorous teacher preparation programs must be based on careful consideration of what excellent teachers do when they enter the classroom. A central claim is that rigorous teacher preparation programs require teacher candidates to adapt their knowledge and expertise appropriately when facing various classroom situations. Teacher candidates learn this skill through literacy course work.

Rigorous literacy teacher preparation requires teacher candidates to be immersed in solving complicated literacy problems such as listening to a student read and deciding which literacy skills and strategies to teach and to make choices among the many different ways to address the student's literacy problems. This type of thinking requires the use of literacy theory, knowledge of literacy processes, and problem-solving capabilities that elevates the work of teacher preparation programs to a high level of rigor.

What Are the U.S. Standards for Rigor in Literacy Teaching?

One source of expert opinion about what it means to be an excellent teacher is the National Board for Professional Teaching Standards (NBPTS). The NBPTS (2004) has articulated standards and an assessment process for ascertaining whether or not experienced teachers have reached those standards. Implicit in the NBPTS standards is the integration of four kinds of knowledge:

1. theoretical knowledge about child development, content, and curriculum;
2. expertise in teaching and assessment;
3. communication with stakeholders; and
4. ongoing professional development.

The NBPTS standards are meant for the evaluation of experienced teachers—teachers who choose to develop an extensive teaching portfolio of their work, including videotapes, student work, and reflections about what they are doing and why. These standards provide a way to judge the work of excellent teachers and determine who should receive NBPTS credentials.

For the evaluation of novice teacher candidates, the Interstate New Teacher Assessment and Support Consortium (INTASC) standards (1992) promote the same kind of rigor as the NBPTS standards do for experienced teachers. The INTASC standards also address the same principles as the NBPTS. The INTASC standards are as follows:

- Standard 1: knowledge of subject (subject matter),
- Standard 2: learning and human development (student learning),
- Standard 3: adapting instruction (diverse learners),
- Standard 4: strategies (instructional strategies),
- Standard 5: motivation and management (learning environment),
- Standard 6: communication skills (communication),
- Standard 7: planning (planning instruction),
- Standard 8: assessment,
- Standard 9: commitment (reflection and professional development), and
- Standard 10: partnerships (collaboration, ethics, and relationships).

Many U.S. universities hold their teacher candidates accountable to these standards through the development of a program portfolio and final exit conference. The teacher candidates complete portfolios and conferences, in addition to classroom experiences, to demonstrate their ability to be reflective and to articulate their knowledge. Through application and articulation, teacher candidates provide documentation for others to deem them prepared for the classroom.

Literacy teacher educators have a similar set of standards to use in the development of literacy programs for beginning teachers. The International Reading Association (IRA) has developed and published *Standards for Reading Professionals—Revised 2003*. Although these standards are intended for novice teachers, they are consistent with the standards of the NBPTS. IRA's standards are as follows:

1. Candidates have knowledge of the foundations of reading and writing processes and instruction.
2. Candidates use a wide range of instructional practices, approaches, methods, and curriculum materials to support reading and writing instruction.
3. Candidates use a variety of assessment tools and practices to plan and evaluate effective reading instruction.
4. Candidates create a literate environment that fosters reading and writing by integrating foundational knowledge, use of instructional practices, approaches and methods, curriculum materials, and the appropriate use of assessments.

5. Candidates view professional development as a career-long effort and responsibility. (p. 8)

These three sets of standards require teachers and teacher candidates to achieve the rigorous goal of integrating theory and practice.

How Are Teacher Preparation Programs Designed to Address Professional Standards?

How Do We Know Rigor When We See It?

The theory-to-practice decision-making process often has been conceptualized as a reflective teaching cycle and is a useful way to conceptualize these standards in action (Mallow & Patterson, 1999; Stephens, 1990).

Figure 3.1 summarizes that processes in six steps, or phases, of the complex and recursive cycle that integrates thought and action in the context of instructional decision making. This figure is a graphic representation of a teaching and learning cycle and demonstrates what excellent teachers must do as they negotiate the unpredictable and complex realities of the classroom. This cycle illustrates that rigorous teaching is much more than simply reading a script or following a set of predetermined steps. It requires thoughtful consideration of options, anticipating possible consequences, and holding multiple contingencies in mind as student responses unfold. This is what rigorous teacher preparation programs must prepare novice teachers to do— strategically adapt knowledge and expertise when facing novel classroom situations (Daggett, 2004; Iran-Nejad, McKeachie, & Berliner, 1990). Although teacher preparation programs across the United States differ somewhat in accordance to local contexts and state certification requirements, many programs use some version of this reflective teaching cycle to design course activities and field experiences to prepare literacy teachers.

Rigor in a Literacy Assessment Course

The following excerpt shows an example of a novice teacher's response to a challenging experience in one teacher preparation program. This program operates in a large state university in the southern part of the United States. These descriptions include an excerpt from a teacher candidate's written work, written reflections, and explanations that provide a glimpse into experiences that typically happen in one of the last three semesters of a

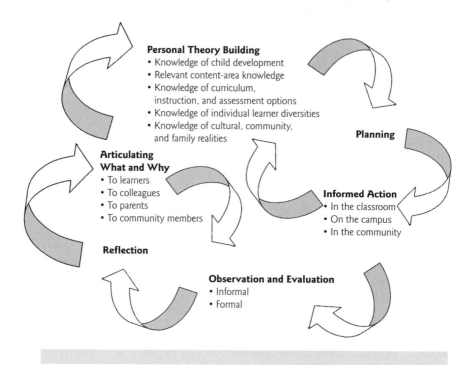

Personal Theory Building
• Knowledge of child development
• Relevant content-area knowledge
• Knowledge of curriculum,
  instruction, and assessment options
• Knowledge of individual learner diversities
• Knowledge of cultural, community,
  and family realities

Planning

**Articulating
What and Why**
• To learners
• To colleagues
• To parents
• To community members

Informed Action
• In the classroom
• On the campus
• In the community

Reflection

Observation and Evaluation
• Informal
• Formal

teacher preparation program in a literacy assessment course and an initial
field experience.

As part of their undergraduate studies in many teacher preparation
programs, teacher candidates are required to take a literacy assessment course
and tutor a student in the grade that they plan to teach. Generally, teacher
candidates have had one or two foundational education courses by this
point, but they may or may not have had a hands-on component similar to
this course. During the semester-long course, teacher candidates learn a
variety of informal literacy assessments, administer the assessments to a
student, plan lessons to address their student's strengths and needs, and then
reflect on the lesson to plan for the next one. In this excerpt, teacher
candidate Lisa Davidson writes about her ninth lesson with Kylie, a first-
grade student. (*Note*: Brackets denote the professor's explanations.)

Planning

Writing

- Time to finish cat book
- Work on vocabulary and sentences
- Discuss cover

Read-Aloud

- *Playing Right Field* (Welch, 1995)

Strategies

- I will monitor Kylie's writing and assess it after tutoring.

Taking Action

[*Lisa implements her lesson.*]

Observing/Evaluating

Notes during the lesson indicate that Kylie finished her book and took it home. During the book reading, Kylie wrote the word *reverie* in her dictionary. I will use the sheet to assess Kylie's writing, but I think this is the most difficult assessment I have made.

Reflecting

[*Lisa's reflection of the lesson is as follows. In it we see how Lisa has begun to articulate what she is doing and why she is doing it.*] I am so glad that we did finish the book today. Cats are Kylie's favorite topic and now she has written her own book about them. I feel that I learned a lot about assessing writing by assessing Kylie's story. I am learning what to look for while focusing on the positive aspects of the writing. Kylie did a good job overall! She has a theme and her writing has purpose. She varied the content while focusing on Pickles, the cat. Kylie is definitely an emergent writer because she makes a lot of approximations while spelling. She did use clauses and some varied sentence structure. She did not, however, use other elements of syntax. The only immediate instructional need that Kylie appears to have is for the use of consistent punctuation to separate her sentences.

At Kylie's request, I read *Playing Right Field* (Welch, 1995) at the end. Kylie laughed at all of the places where she laughed the last time. At her choice she wrote the word *reverie* in her vocabulary book. I am glad that she is using this tool.

Theory Building

[*In the last section of her reflection, Lisa is making decisions about what might help Kylie next. This aids the reader of the selection to see what Lisa thinks is important for the student and the teacher.*] It might be a good idea to have Kylie read her story aloud and place periods where her voice stops. Since Kylie uses mostly basic vocabulary words in her writing, she would benefit from more books that contain descriptive adverbs and adjectives. Then she could see what other authors do. I am very proud of all the effort that Kylie showed as she wrote her story. She seems to really enjoy writing and gets excited about it. I think that Kylie is an extremely promising emergent writer. I wish I had more time to work with her. I feel that I have learned a great deal and I am grateful to Kylie for helping me learn. (Lisa Davidson, personal communication, November 14, 1997)

In this example, after analyzing writing samples, Lisa discusses Kylie's learning as her own learning. She not only describes Kylie's work but also is able to provide examples of it to assign a level of proficiency. While her time with Kylie is ending, Lisa continues to make statements of what needs to happen next for her student. She understands the connection of reading and writing as she addresses them together. This was typical of how Lisa integrated theory and practice.

Teaching Rigor

At each point in this teaching and learning cycle, teacher candidates must be held accountable for using what they know about learners, content, and the school and community context to make appropriate instructional decisions in the midst of classroom problems. As teacher educators observe and listen to each teacher candidate during field experiences and read their reflective writing on these experiences, they expect teacher candidates to be deliberate with decisions and demonstrate use of their knowledge. Although teacher candidates may be able to use their knowledge to pass tests and write papers, rigor for literacy teacher candidates goes beyond these pencil-and-paper measures. It means that they can effectively apply their learning to real classrooms and real students.

Conclusion

Rigorous literacy teacher preparation programs call for teacher candidates to be immersed in "complex" problems, to learn to see coherent patterns across complex situations, and to choose the most feasible and most productive actions. Rigor in teacher preparation programs is about having teacher educators and school-based practicing teachers support teacher candidates as they learn to solve those problems and as they build the confidence to face unfamiliar situations. Rigor in such a context is different from the widely used notion of rigor that denotes "difficult content." Rigor in a program that prepares literacy teachers demands the strategic and purposeful integration of theory and practice, difficult concepts, and the thoughtful application of these concepts.

REFERENCES

Daggett, W.R. (2004). *The rigor/relevance framework*. Retrieved May 17, 2004, from http://www.daggett.com

International Reading Association (IRA). (2003). *Standards for reading professionals—Revised 2003*. Newark, DE: Author.

Interstate New Teacher Assessment and Support Consortium (INTASC). (1992). *Model standards for beginning teacher licensing and development: A resource for state dialogue* [Electronic version]. Washington, DC: Council of Chief State School Officers. Retrieved August 30, 2005, from http://www.ccsso.org/projects/interstate_new_teacher_assessment_ and_support_consortium

Iran-Nejad, A., McKeachie, W., & Berliner, D.C. (1990). The multisource nature of learning: An introduction. *Review of Educational Research*, 60(4), 509–515.

Mallow, F., & Patterson, L. (1999). *Framing literacy: Teaching/learning in K–8 classrooms.* Norwood, MA: Christopher-Gordon.

National Board for Professional Teaching Standards (NBPTS). (2004). *National Board for Professional Teaching Standards Candidate Resource Center.* Retrieved May 17, 2003, from http://www.nbpts.org/candidates

Papson, S. (1995). The rhetoric of rigor: Administrative incursions into pedagogy. *National Social Science Perspectives Journal*, 7(2), 2–15.

Stephens, D. (1990). *What matters? A primer for teaching reading.* Portsmouth, NH: Heinemann.

LITERATURE CITED

Welch, W. (1995). *Playing right field.* Ill. M. Simont. New York: Scholastic.

Teacher Preparation Programs Make a Difference in Teacher Candidates' Perspectives About Literacy Teaching

KAREN E. SMITH AND CAROLE S. RHODES

❖ ❖ ❖

Teacher preparation programs prepare teacher candidates to enter their profession ready to teach literacy, and they require candidates to change many of their preconceived perceptions of literacy education. Effective literacy teachers model valuable literacy practices as their teaching identities develop over time. Excellent literacy teacher preparation programs promote teacher candidates' independent visions of what literacy is, what quality teaching consists of, and what the notion of lifelong professional teacher preparation consists of. Well-prepared literacy teachers continue to work toward improving their own literacy skills while promoting literacy in diverse settings.

Effective teacher preparation programs develop novice teachers who may become literacy leaders. These novice teachers use research to improve their teaching practices and to help develop into change agents for educational reform. Teacher candidates who are well prepared in teaching literacy are confident in their knowledge of literacy practices and comfortable about effectively teaching reading to diverse student populations in various settings.

❖ ❖ ❖

CHAPTER HIGHLIGHTS

◆ Teacher candidates develop a literacy identity that is part of learning to become a confident literacy teacher.

◆ Teacher candidates attend course work that encourages new teachers to become leaders.

◆ Literacy teacher preparation helps teacher candidates develop a solid vision of quality literacy teaching that supports the use of effectively modeled literacy strategies.

◆ Literacy teacher preparation programs launch the notion of lifelong learning in an ever-advancing world of literacy education.

LEARNING HOW TO TEACH LITERACY

When Shirley, a teacher candidate, begins her first year of teacher preparation, she quickly realizes that she can no longer fake her way through reading and writing. One of her first journal-writing assignments includes an entry describing how difficult the literacy methods courses are for her. She writes,

> This course is tough. I don't think of myself as a *model* reader or writer, and I've never before really thought about how one comes to learn to read and write. Guess I better start now. I don't want my students to think I'm illiterate! Before I took this course, I never really thought beyond what I write. Doing it [reading and writing] yourself is different from being the teacher in charge. I'd like to know more about ways that I can motivate students to read and write so they don't miss out. You can fake it when you're writing your own stuff but when you're teaching...well, that's a different matter. I have thoroughly enjoyed this class. It has changed the way I think about literacy in more ways than you can imagine.

Shirley is typical of many teacher candidates who learn in teacher preparation that they must become models of literacy.

eacher candidates' professional identities are built around the idea of fostering a literate society. Teacher preparation programs are filled with experiences designed to transform teacher candidates' notions about how they were previously taught and how those prior experiences will affect them as they take on the role of influencing the literacy of a nation (American Association of Colleges for Teacher Education, 2004).

The journey through a teacher preparation program is demanding because teacher candidates must improve their own literacy skills and learn how to support the literacy learning of the diverse learners they will encounter during their teaching careers. Extensive reorganization of teacher preparation programs in the past two decades has been a response to higher expectations for the education system, increased demands for workers to have literacy skills prior to entering the job market, and higher expectations for literacy across the United States.

Recent Changes to Teacher Preparation Programs

Teacher preparation is at both the forefront of reforming how students learn to be literate and the forefront of transforming the literacy levels of society. One of the greatest changes to teacher preparation programs in the past two decades has been the revising of literacy methods courses (Simmons & Carroll, 2003; Smith & Stock, 2003). Reforms in methods courses include engaging in new literacies studies as technology becomes a greater part of literacy learning and the concept of literacy itself changes. In addition, literacy methods courses have become more integrated with experiences in the field. The International Reading Association's (IRA) National Commission on Excellence in Elementary Teacher Preparation for Reading Instruction (2003b) found that effective teacher preparation programs comprise of an extensive curriculum that fosters strong literacy knowledge and literacy experiences in the field; a vision of high standards and practices; and a learning environment that includes the students, university faculty, and school district mentors (Maloch, Fine, & Flint, 2002/2003). Revision of literacy methods courses provides a greater opportunity for candidates to become better literacy teachers and a greater chance that they will improve practice in the field after they graduate.

Teacher preparation programs have become transformative for teaching candidates in light of certification reforms and the emphasis on literacy education (Porter, Youngs, & Odden, 2001). The breadth and depth of literacy skills required of teachers currently in the field makes it necessary that there be a great deal of rigor in literacy methods courses to prepare candidates to be "field ready" on the day they begin teaching. Rigor imposed by teacher educators stems from their urgency to make an impact on teacher candidates; otherwise, school change is undermined by practices that sustain current structures (Murray, 1996). Britzman (2003) describes the phenomenon of merely introducing teacher candidates to current school culture as practice makes practice, also the title of her book. In order to make a change that advances current teaching practices, there must be transformative education programs challenging the normalization of sustained teaching methods. Progress and reform in teacher preparation are clearly connected to reform of literacy education as it permeates all levels and curricular areas in teaching.

Changing literacy practices in general and greater pressure from governments and the public have raised the bar for teacher preparation and literacy education (American Association of Colleges for Teacher Education, 2004; Darling-Hammond, 2001; National Council for Accreditation of Teacher Education, 2004). Admissions requirements for teacher preparation programs have been raised. Entrance grade point averages for teacher candidates are higher than in most other programs in colleges and universities. Entrance requirements include tests of literacy and numeracy. There also are increased numbers of programs requiring teacher candidates to earn a degree before they enter teacher preparation. Programs also emphasize more liaisons with schools to ensure a collaborative integration of professional development and school improvement. Thus, candidates are required to demonstrate literacy teaching competence much sooner, before they are hired.

Standards for teacher preparation programs have gone up and, in turn, the standards for teacher licensing, certification, and assessment have risen, increasing educational requirements and putting pressure on institutions with these programs and those in the field who partner with teacher educators (Darling-Hammond, 2001). With higher admissions requirements, more skills to master, higher and more levels of competence to aspire to, and more public scrutiny, the rigor in teacher preparation programs has increased. Teacher educators, and those with whom they work, including teacher candidates and field experience associates, have immense pressure to do better and work harder. In literacy methods courses, that means setting clear goals for teacher educators as they become literacy leaders and change agents for new research-based literacy methods.

Teacher Candidates as Literacy Leaders

In teacher preparation programs, teacher candidates learn what research indicates about literacy education, and they also learn that they have the important dual role of exciting students about reading and assessing student performance (American Association of Colleges for Teacher Education, 2002). Each role influences the other. Of course, maintaining this delicate balance has long-term consequences for students and the perception of their literacy skills (Applebee, 2003). Therefore, teacher candidates must do more than prepare themselves for what is currently in the field; they must prepare to become change agents for improved literacy in an evolving literacy world that is influenced by emerging technologies and greater mixes of languages.

The everyday work of teacher educators is to inspire emerging teachers to become literacy leaders (McAndrew, 2005). Being literacy leaders means learning to be a model of and motivator for literacy; working with diverse levels of literacy and multiple cultures; understanding and using many types of literacy assessment and evaluation; understanding, using, and interpreting education research; and becoming an innovator for continued literacy improvement (see, for example, Wepner, Strickland, & Feeley, 2002).

Being Models of and Motivators in Literacy

Teacher candidates must improve their personal levels of literacy and their knowledge about how that process happens. When teacher candidates take their first courses in teaching, they often are troubled by their lack of knowledge about how students learn to be literate. Many teacher candidates have gone through life just being literate, questioning neither how that came about for them nor how that comes about for others. Their "teacher identity" formation begins with thinking about their personal levels of literacy and refining their skills to become better literacy models for students. They learn to write better, read more, and adopt the integration of technology into their literacy discourses (Adsit, 2004). In portfolios and through course work, teacher candidates learn to monitor their own literacy skills so they can be models in their classrooms. They learn that there are very few students who grew up exactly as they did or who learn in the same ways they do. By recognizing these issues, teacher candidates learn to shift the emphasis from themselves to their students.

Many of the students with whom teacher candidates work must first be motivated to read and write. Candidates must learn how to encourage students' recreational reading, develop students' literacy skills, and improve students' comprehension in content areas. Teacher candidates learn that their students must have active engagement with reading materials in order to develop as readers and respond to texts. They learn that assigning reading and responding to reading through writing are only small pieces of the greater range of skills that promote active engagement with learning materials (Cunningham, 2003; Hillocks & Smith, 2003; Power, 1997).

Working With Diverse Learners and Struggling Readers

Teacher preparation programs help candidates learn that diversity among students does not have to be a frustrating experience and that differentiated instruction and innovative classroom methodologies support a diverse community of learners. Diversity among students can be in the form of struggling readers who may be missing skills, alliterate students who may not be self-motivated, students who are developmentally challenged or have a range of skills levels and backgrounds, and students who have specific work preferences and abilities (Spiegel, 2002; Yokota & Teale, 2002).

Literacy methods courses provide teacher candidates with background knowledge, such as recognizing the special needs of students with disabilities and using alternative teaching methods and differentiated instruction, which is considered necessary for recognizing and addressing the needs of diverse learners in their classrooms. Candidates learn about strategies that will support a diversity of learners and struggling readers and writers so that when these candidates are starting their teaching careers, students in danger of failing, students who have been excluded in the past from instruction (because their special needs could not be included in regular instruction), and students, who would otherwise be indistinguishable, are recognized and supported through instructional scaffolding (Moore & Hinchman, 2003; Vacca & Vacca, 2004).

Working With Multiple Cultures and a Global Society

The reality of today's classrooms is that diversity goes beyond abilities and backgrounds. In literacy methods courses, candidates become familiar with multicultural literature and instructional strategies for English-language learners (Applebee & Purves, 1992; Hudelson, Poyner, & Wolfe, 2003). Teacher candidates also learn to value literature from many cultures, and they learn how to bring these materials into the classroom to facilitate meaningful interactions with text (Fox & Short, 2003; Grisham, 2000).

Today, the fastest growing population of students in the United States consists of students who come from homes in which English is not the only language spoken (Slavin & Cheung, 2004). As a result, English-language programs are growing at a rapid rate, and literacy methods courses are increasingly attending to the needs of a global society in which classrooms are multicultural. Teacher preparation programs do not ignore this phenomenon, and literacy methods instruct teacher candidates on how to teach English and support students without undermining their native language and culture.

Understanding and Using Many Levels of Literacy Assessment and Evaluation

Assessment and evaluation are complex topics discussed in literacy methods courses. The topics are complex, for example, because students are growing, learning, and constantly changing; students' learning styles and preferences, coupled with their abilities, are challenging to ascertain in a system of growth; and the dichotomy of motivating students as opposed to assessing them is delicate and must be balanced. It is common for teacher candidates to question the wisdom of what at first looks like a trial-and-error approach. However, teacher candidates, through their field experiences in collaborating schools, soon learn that the needs of students must be served through assessment and evaluation (Massey, 2003).

Teacher candidates learn about leveled texts and assessing both the readability of texts and the reading levels of students. They learn how to plan interventions, select appropriate strategies, and select reading materials based on matching students with challenging, appropriate texts. They examine the science and the art of connecting assessments of materials, learning situations, and student capabilities. In addition, they learn the differences between assessment and evaluation and between authentic assessment and standardized testing, and they learn to value both process and product of reading and writing. Literacy methods courses integrate the uses of testing to inform instruction; therefore, they play a key role in helping emerging teachers to develop a sense of informed, professional decision making, instead of relying solely on their instincts (Baines & Farrell, 2003; Clandinin & Connelly, 1992).

Understanding, Using, and Interpreting Education Research

Literacy methods have been the source of much educational debate. From the "reading wars" of the past decades to the "reading research wars" of the 21st century (Flippo, 1999; Stanovich, 1990, 2000), very few other educational issues have drawn so much attention. The debates may appear to demonstrate that educators have not found answers to important questions through research; however, like science and medical researchers, educators should reserve judgment and accept that the research demonstrates what educators currently know.

Literacy methods courses help teacher candidates to understand, use, and interpret education research for the purpose of making informed decisions about their classroom activities. These courses both teach how research can be used to inform instruction and caution beginning teachers to think about the consequences of the actions they take. Methods courses provide teacher candidates with opportunities to discuss the nature of the system they are entering and to develop their skills as critical thinkers (Smith & Stock, 2003).

Being Innovators and Change Agents for Continued Literacy Educational Improvement

Many changes to literacy methods courses in the past two decades have caused dramatic shifts in how teacher educators teach literacy. First, in effective teacher preparation programs, literacy methods are integrated and conceptually connected to the study of all subject areas as educators have developed language-to-learn strategies and methodologies for all subjects (Vacca & Vacca, 2004). Second, viewing and representing have been added (Begoray & Morin, 2002) to the list of language skills that previously encompassed only reading, writing, listening, and speaking. Third, technology has dramatically changed the ways that people interact with text (Bruce & Levin, 2003), and new genres and forms of communication have emerged through digital technologies. As these changes have occurred, literacy courses have adopted them and transformed accordingly.

Through the continual transformation of literacy, teacher preparation programs have had to become innovative. Teacher educators have had to learn to adopt new research and technologies, adapt to the changing nature of literacy, and consequently, work more collaboratively with schools so innovations become feasible in schools. As well, teacher educators have had to stay abreast of technological changes at just the right pace so as not to be too far ahead or too far behind (see, for example, Mallette & Karchmer, 2002). Technology use increases the demand for a more literate society (Karsenti & Thiber, 2002).

From the time of Sputnik's launch in 1957 to the publication of the highly discussed *A Nation at Risk: The Imperative for Educational Reform* (The National Commission on Excellence in Education, 1983), several groups have devoted considerable efforts to educational reform (Darling-Hammond, 1998, 1999, 2001; Goodlad, 1991; Hess, Rotherdam, & Walsh, 2004). Scholars, policymakers, teacher preparation institutions, and legislators have made an effort to bring about changes in teacher preparation programs. The No Child Left Behind Act of 2001—signed into law in January 2002—is yet another marker in education reform intended to ensure that teacher quality, although defined somewhat differently, remains a priority. Historically and today, educational reform focuses on literacy education.

Teacher preparation programs are rigorous because there is a high emphasis on literacy methods that are both complex to learn about and to implement. Along with rigor is the satisfaction that comes from teacher candidates experiencing high levels of learning and becoming transformed through their literacy methods courses.

Conclusion

Effective teacher preparation programs make a difference in the lives of teacher candidates by preparing them for ever-increasing levels of rigor and encouraging them to form professional identities. These programs also affect teacher candidates far into the future by making them lifelong learners.

Literacy education is the foundation for the differences made in teacher candidates' lives. There are high expectations and immense demands, in addition to rigorous entrance requirements, on teacher educators as they prepare the next generation of teachers. Well-prepared novice teachers, as noted in chapter 1, are confident in their knowledge and instructional practices, while "teachers who are less prepared expressed their frustration at the disconnect between their training and their teaching" (IRA, 2003a, p. 7).

Teacher preparation programs cannot merely produce future teachers and leave the job of lifelong learning to someone else. Teacher preparation courses give teacher candidates their first glimpse of learning what it takes to be a teacher and of the corresponding responsibilities to a literate society. Teacher educators must inspire teacher candidates to continue learning, to thirst constantly for new knowledge, and to believe in the importance of literacy as it evolves in an environment where technology constantly changes how society reads and writes (Kinzer & Leander, 2003). Teacher educators also must be models and motivators for their students because they will help the students read and be successful in an increasingly high-stakes standard-setting environment. The impact of teacher preparation is ubiquitous; therefore, teacher preparation programs must be strong and strategic to literacy development.

Teacher educators cannot expect that teacher candidates merely graduate once from colleges and universities. The partnership between teacher preparation programs and teachers perhaps ends at retirement. It is a career-long endeavor. The impact of teacher preparation is everywhere and cyclical from students to the work force. The point where change effectively can be made is when teacher candidates arrive for their initial preparation, in which they expect to be transformed and challenged, and in which they have wide-eyed hopes of becoming the best at what they aspire to do—to teach a nation to be literate by being models of literacy themselves.

REFERENCES

Adsit, J.N. (2004). *A report on technology-mediated professional development programs: For teachers and school leaders.* Washington, DC: American Association of Colleges for Teacher Education Publications.

American Association of Colleges for Teacher Education. (2002). *Research-based literacy instruction: Implications for teacher education* [Electronic version]. Washington, DC: Author. Retrieved April 29, 2005, from http://www.aacte.org/about_us/literacy.pdf

American Association of Colleges for Teacher Education. (2004). *Teacher education primer 2004: Information for members of Congress for the reauthorization of higher education* [Electronic version]. Washington, DC: Author. Retrieved June 30, 2004, from http://www.aacte.org/Governmental_Relations/04primer.pdf

Applebee, A.N. (2003). Balancing the curriculum in the English language arts: Exploring the components of effective teaching and learning. In J. Flood, D. Lapp, J.R. Squire, & J.M. Jensen (Eds.), *Handbook of research on teaching the English language arts* (2nd ed., pp. 676–684). Mahwah, NJ: Erlbaum.

Applebee, A.N., & Purves, A.C. (1992). Literature and the English language arts. In P.W. Jackson (Ed.), *Handbook of research on curriculum: A project of the American Educational Research Association* (pp. 726–748). New York: Macmillan.

Baines, L., & Farrell, E.J. (2003). The Tao of instructional models. In J. Flood, D. Lapp, J.R. Squire, & J.M. Jensen (Eds.), *Handbook of research on teaching the English language arts* (2nd ed., pp. 74–86). Mahwah, NJ: Erlbaum.

Begoray, D.L., & Morin, F. (2002). Multiple literacies in language arts: Sustainable teacher change through a summer institute. *Reading Online, 6*(4). Retrieved July 11, 2005, from http://www.readingonline.org/articles/art_index.asp?HREF=/articles/begoray

Britzman, D.P. (2003). *Practice makes practice: A critical study of learning to teach.* Albany, NY: State University of New York Press.

Bruce, B., & Levin, J. (2003). Roles for new technologies in language arts: Inquiry, communication, construction, and expression. In J. Flood, D. Lapp, J.R. Squire, & J.M. Jensen (Eds.), *Handbook of research on teaching the English language arts* (2nd ed., pp. 649–657). Mahwah, NJ: Erlbaum.

Clandinin, D.J., & Connelly, F.M. (1992). Teacher as curriculum maker. In P.W. Jackson (Ed.), *Handbook of research on curriculum: A project of the American Educational Research Association* (pp. 363–401). New York: Macmillan.

Cunningham, A.E. (2003). Reading matters: How reading engagement influences cognition. In J. Flood, D. Lapp, J.R. Squire, & J.M. Jensen (Eds.), *Handbook of research on teaching the English language arts* (2nd ed., pp. 666–675). Mahwah, NJ: Erlbaum.

Darling-Hammond, L. (1998, September). *How can we ensure a caring, competent, qualified teacher for every child? Strategies for solving the dilemmas of teacher supply, demand, and standards.* Paper presented at the meeting of the American Federation of Teachers/National Education Association, Washington, DC. Retrieved November 30, 2003, from http://www.middleweb.com/TchRcrtLDH.html

Darling-Hammond, L. (with La Fors, J., & Snyder, J.). (1999). *Educating teachers for California's future: A teacher education summit of California college and university presidents*. San Francisco: The Irvine Foundation.

Darling-Hammond, L. (2001). *The right to learn: A blueprint for creating schools that work*. San Francisco: Jossey-Bass.

Flippo, R.F. (1999). Redefining the reading wars: The war against reading researchers. *Educational Leadership, 57*(2), 39–41.

Fox, D.L., & Short, K.G. (Eds.). (2003). *Stories matter: The complexity of cultural authenticity in children's literature*. Urbana, IL: National Council of Teachers of English.

Goodlad, J.I. (1991). Better teachers for our nation's schools. *Education Digest, 56*(6), 3–5.

Grisham, D.L. (2000). Connecting theoretical conceptions of reading to practice: A longitudinal study of elementary school teachers. *Reading Psychology, 21*(2), 145–170.

Hess, M.F., Rotherdam, J.A., & Walsh, K. (Eds.). (2004). *A qualified teacher in every classroom? Appraising old answers and new ideas*. Cambridge, MA: Harvard Education.

Hillocks, G., & Smith, M.W. (2003). Grammars and literacy learning. In J. Flood, D. Lapp, J.R. Squire, & J.M. Jensen (Eds.), *Handbook of research on teaching the English language arts* (2nd ed., pp. 721–737). Mahwah, NJ: Erlbaum.

Hudelson, S., Poyner, L., & Wolfe, P. (2003). Teaching bilingual and ESL children and adolescents. In J. Flood, D. Lapp, J.R. Squire, & J.M. Jensen (Eds.), *Handbook of research on teaching the English language arts* (2nd ed., pp. 421–434). Mahwah, NJ: Erlbaum.

International Reading Association (IRA). (2003a). *Executive summary of the National Commission on Excellence in Elementary Teacher Preparation for Reading Instruction*. Retrieved April 22, 2005, from http://www.reading.org/downloads/resources/1061teacher_ed_com_summary.pdf

International Reading Association (IRA). (2003b). *Prepared to make a difference: Research evidence on how some of America's best college programs prepare teachers of reading*. Newark, DE: Author.

Karsenti, T., & Thiber, G. (2002). *Teaching educational research to student teachers: The pros and cons of using information and communication technology*. Montreal, QC: University of Montreal. (ERIC Document Reproduction Service No. ED482000)

Kinzer, C.K., & Leander, K. (2003). Technology and the language arts: Implication of an expanded definition of literacy. In J. Flood, D. Lapp. J.R. Squire, & J.M. Jensen (Eds.), *Handbook of research on teaching the English language arts* (2nd ed., pp. 546–565). Mahwah, NJ: Erlbaum.

Mallette, M.H., & Karchmer, R.A. (2002). Lessons learned from preparing preservice teachers to integrate technology in their literacy teaching. In D.L. Schallert, C.M. Fairbanks, J. Worthy, B. Maloch, & J.V. Hoffman (Eds.), *Fifty-first yearbook of the National Reading Conference* (pp. 298–309). Chicago: National Reading Conference.

Maloch, B., Fine, J., & Flint, A.S. (2002/2003). "I just feel like I'm ready": Exploring the influence of quality teacher preparation on beginning teachers. *The Reading Teacher, 56*, 348–350.

Massey, D.D. (2003). A comprehension checklist: What if it doesn't make sense? *The Reading Teacher, 57*, 81–84.

McAndrew, D.A. (2005). *Literacy leadership: Six strategies for peoplework*. Newark, DE: International Reading Association.

Moore, D.W., & Hinchman, K.A. (2003). *Starting out: A guide to teaching adolescents who struggle with reading*. Boston: Allyn & Bacon.

Murray, F.B. (1996). Beyond natural teaching: The case for professional education. In F.B. Murray (Ed.), *The teacher educator's handbook: Building a knowledge base for the preparation of teachers* (pp. 3–13). San Francisco: Jossey-Bass.

The National Commission on Excellence in Education. (1983). *A nation at risk: The imperative for educational reform*. Washington, DC: U.S. Department of Education. Retrieved June 6, 2005, from http://www.ed.gov/pubs/NatAtRisk/title.html

National Council for Accreditation of Teacher Education. (2004). *Quick facts*. Retrieved June 30, 2004, from http://www.ncate.org/ncate/fact_sheet.htm

No Child Left Behind Act of 2001, Pub. L. No. 107-110, 115 Stat. 1425 (2002).

Porter, A.C., Youngs, P., & Odden, A. (2001). Advances in teacher assessments and their uses. In V. Richardson (Ed.), *Handbook of research on teaching* (4th ed., pp. 259–297). Washington, DC: American Educational Research Association.

Power, B.M. (1997). *Long roads, short distances: Teaching writing and writing teachers*. Portsmouth, NH: Heinemann.

Simmons, J., & Carroll, P.S. (2003). Today's middle grades: Different structures, students, and classrooms. In J. Flood, D. Lapp, J.R. Squire, & J.M. Jensen (Eds.), *Handbook of research on teaching the English language arts* (2nd ed., pp. 357–392). Mahwah, NJ: Erlbaum.

Slavin, R.E., & Cheung, A. (2004). How do English-language learners learn to read? *Educational Leadership*, *61*(6), 52–57.

Smith, K., & Stock, P.L. (2003). Trends and issues in research in the teaching of the English language arts. In J. Flood, D. Lapp. J.R. Squire, & J.M. Jensen (Eds.), *Handbook of research on teaching the English language arts* (2nd ed., pp. 114–130). Mahwah, NJ: Erlbaum.

Spiegel, H.A.L. (2002, June). *Pre-service teacher training and implementation in the classroom: Consideration*. San Antonio, TX: National Educational Computer Conference Proceedings. (ERIC Document Reproduction Service No. ED475952)

Stanovich, K.E. (1990). A call for the end to the paradigm wars in reading research. *Journal of Reading Behavior*, *22*(3), 221–231.

Stanovich, K.E. (2000). *Progress in understanding reading: Scientific foundations and new frontiers*. New York: Guilford.

Vacca, R.T., & Vacca, J.A.L. (2004). *Content area reading: Literacy and learning across the curriculum* (8th ed.). Boston: Pearson/Allyn & Bacon.

Wepner, S.B., Strickland, D.S., & Feeley, J.T. (Eds.) (2002). *The administration and supervision of reading programs* (3rd ed.). New York: Teachers College Press.

Yokota, J., & Teale, W.H. (2002). Literacy development for culturally diverse populations. In S.B. Wepner, D.S. Strickland, & J.T. Feeley (Eds.), *Administration and supervision of reading programs* (3rd ed., pp. 153–165). New York: Teachers College Press.

TRUTH 5

Teacher Preparation Programs Offer Targeted Field Experiences in Literacy

SUSAN DAVIS LENSKI AND SUSAN L. NIERSTHEIMER

Quality literacy teaching results from a combination of factors, including a careful balance of course work and field experiences. These factors help teacher candidates understand and apply foundational knowledge during literacy instruction. The union of theory and practice is critical to teaching literacy well; both experiences help teacher candidates apply best-practice principles to teaching situations.

Because field experiences are a crucial component of teacher candidate education, teacher preparation programs provide in-school experiences for their teacher candidates. Teacher educators search out field experiences that provide literacy environments that complement the course work offered in the teacher preparation program. These in-school experiences are used as real-life examples of the theory and practice that teacher candidates learn in teacher preparation courses.

Literacy Teacher Preparation: Ten Truths Teacher Educators Need to Know by Susan Davis Lenski, Dana L. Grisham, and Linda S. Wold, Editors. Copyright © 2006 by the International Reading Association.

CHAPTER HIGHLIGHTS

◆ Field experiences are opportunities for teacher candidates to observe classroom teachers and to teach in supervised settings.

◆ Field experiences are orchestrated through teacher preparation programs.

◆ Professional organizations recognize the value of field experiences in teacher preparation programs.

◆ Research indicates that teacher candidates of excellent teacher preparation programs use field experiences as a tool for further learning about teaching literacy.

◆ Teacher candidates need both field experiences and literacy methods courses to prepare them to be quality literacy teachers.

LEARNING BY TEACHING

"I love teaching. I absolutely love it!" Emily, a teacher candidate, bursts into her literacy methods class with her face glowing.

Emily and her classmates had just spent four weeks in an urban school during a university-directed field experience. During those four weeks, Emily was able to work with Mrs. Foster, one of the best second-grade teachers in the school district. Emily was able to observe Mrs. Foster preparing lessons, managing guided literacy centers, conferring with students in a writers' workshop, and teaching students how to choose books for independent reading. Mrs. Foster is experienced with teacher candidates who are in their first field experience and she made Emily feel comfortable by introducing her to the students. Once Emily was able to see "real children," she began to understand the teaching methods she had learned in her university courses. Throughout the four weeks, Emily observed and assisted Mrs. Foster, and she taught a guided reading group and developed a literacy center. At the end of the four weeks, the class gave Emily a goodbye party, and each student wrote a card for her. Emily promised that she would return at the end of her semester to volunteer in the classroom. Emily went on to say,

> When I first arrived in Mrs. Foster's class, I was afraid that I wouldn't know what to do. Mrs. Foster asked me to read a story to the class the day I arrived. She gave me a book to read, and luckily it was one that I have read in my college class. Something surprising happened as I was reading to the children. I began to relax and I found myself involved in what I was doing. I wasn't scared or nervous any longer. I was just thinking about the story and the children and how their eyes were alive with learning. I knew that this was the feeling my professors had described when they talked about the joys of teaching.

Teacher candidates sometimes return to literacy methods courses from their field experience placements and report, "I learned more in those four weeks than I did in all my college courses!" Teacher educators know the power of spending time in schools, which is why effective teacher preparation programs offer a variety of field experiences for teacher candidates. In fact, the International Reading Association (2003) surveyed 950 literacy teacher educators and studied eight undergradute programs in depth and found that one of the components of these programs is the notion of apprenticeship—that teacher candidates are given opportunities to spend time in classrooms with mentor teachers. Field experiences are common in accredited teacher preparation programs and are one of the ways in which universities partner with schools to train teacher candidates.

What Are Field Experiences?

Although teacher preparation programs vary widely, all of them require teacher candidates to have field experiences as part of their university requirements. The term *field experiences* covers a variety of school visits that teacher candidates engage in. Early field experiences in effective teacher preparation programs often are structured sessions in which teacher candidates spend time observing excellent literacy teachers. Teacher candidates then return to their university classrooms and discuss what they have observed. As teacher candidates progress through teacher preparation programs, they are provided with additional field experiences. Often, teacher candidates are asked to prepare literacy lessons with mentor teachers, teach small groups, read aloud to the class, design displays, and grade papers and projects. These experiences also are structured so teacher candidates return to university classrooms to discuss their experiences and to help develop their individual teaching styles.

During the last semester of effective teacher preparation programs, teacher candidates are involved with the ultimate field experience—student teaching. During student teaching, teacher candidates spend several weeks to an entire year with a mentor teacher, learning how to apply the literacy theory and practice they have learned in their course work to teach students in schools. Student teaching is an experience in which teacher candidates are able to take increasing amounts of responsibility for the classroom until they progress to teaching the entire school day. Student teaching is the culmination of a teacher preparation program's field experience component; therefore, student teachers are supervised by university personnel and are graded for their abilities as novice teachers.

Balancing Course Work and Field Experiences

Preparing highly qualified new teachers requires a balance of course work and field experiences. The combination of theory and practice produces new teachers who are knowledgeable about content, conversant about pedagogy, and confident in their practices. According to the National Commission on Teaching and America's Future (1996), "What teachers know and can do makes the crucial difference in what teachers can accomplish" (p. 5). Among the common goals of teacher educators is the mentoring of new teachers so they will have a positive impact on student achievement, be more attuned to students' needs, and be able to teach all students (Wise & Leibbrand, 2000).

Excellent models of teacher preparation recognize that there is a core body of knowledge associated with learning to teach that is based on research and best practices. Often, this body of knowledge is assessed by areas of competencies whose foundational elements are the Interstate New Teacher Assessment and Support Consortium principles (1992). These primary competencies, learned during teacher preparation courses, include focusing on and assessing the learner, collaborating with colleagues and the community, providing inclusive education, using a developmental perspective, integrating content and pedagogy, using new and emerging technologies, and adapting instruction to diverse learners.

Professional course work arms teacher candidates with knowledge about the diversity of students at all developmental stages as well as knowledge of what and how to teach. According to Shulman (1986), teachers need to know three areas of content: (1) facts, concepts, theories, and procedures; (2) frameworks that organize and connect ideas; and (3) the rules of evidence and proof. Teacher candidates also need to know how to "teach" this content, or how to get knowledge across to students in socially constructive ways. Instruction in pedagogy provides teacher candidates with ideas on how to structure knowledge so that students in classrooms will learn.

Cochran-Smith and Lytle (1999) add to the understanding of the kinds of knowledge teacher candidates need to be effective. They describe knowledge *for* practice—knowledge learned in textbooks and university classrooms; knowledge *in* practice—knowledge gained via reflection and critical analysis during field experiences; and knowledge *of* practice—knowledge gained from purposeful inquiry. Once teacher candidates acquire foundational teaching knowledge, they can turn their attention to specific subjects such as literacy.

Gaining Knowledge About Literacy Teaching and Learning

Pearson (2003) argues that, as a profession, literacy educators have been too quick to dismiss or overlook the importance of disciplinary knowledge. He believes that teacher preparation programs need to place more emphasis on linguistics, language development, orthography, literature, culture, and the psychology of literacy and learning. Stressing the significance of these disciplines, Pearson believes, would result in better prepared, more effective literacy teachers.

Another study of literacy teacher preparation was conducted by Flippo (1998), who compiled the recommendations of 11 literacy experts about the contexts and practices that facilitate the teaching of reading. The recommendations include combining reading with other language processes; setting up contexts, environments, and purposes for reading; developing or shaping students' perceptions and expectations; using materials effectively; and designing effective literacy lessons. Recommendations for literacy instruction include

> providing multiple, repeated demonstrations of how reading is done or used; planning instruction and individual activities so that, most of the time, students engage in purposeful reading and writing; and using silent reading whenever possible, if appropriate to the purpose. (p. 35)

These contexts and practices can be learned in university settings and applied in classroom settings, but they inevitably include the necessity of teacher candidates acquiring a core body of knowledge. Knowledge about literacy teaching and learning must be gained through organized, reflective study in teacher preparation course work for it to be effectively applied. Teacher candidates cannot intuitively gain such essential knowledge through observations and classroom participation alone.

Coupling Course Work With Field Experiences

With knowledge gained in course work, teacher candidates enter school contexts of field experiences where they can learn by doing. During field experiences, teacher candidates observe mentor teachers, apply their knowledge, test theories, and try out practices in sheltered and supportive environments. To that end, effective teacher preparation programs offer students early and systematic experiences in the field that are deemed vital (e.g., Darling-Hammond, 1990; Haberman, 1996). During field experiences, teacher candidates learn "how to be a teacher rather than simply learning to do the work of a teacher" (Goodfellow & Sumsion, 2000, p. 246). As they spend time in schools watching mentor teachers and trying out ideas, teacher candidates create a repertoire of strategies that they can use when they have their own classrooms. Further, teacher candidates develop their own theory of literacy learning during these experiences (Lenski & Nierstheimer, 2004).

A prototype of a literacy teacher preparation program that links theory and practice is described by Fang and Ashley (2004). These teacher educators created a block of literacy courses in which teacher candidates were "immersed in the learning process through participation in extensive reading, thoughtful discussion, guided practice, critical reflection, and intensive tutoring [of children who had reading and writing needs]" (p. 51). In addition, teacher candidates benefited from modeling provided by both their university instructors and practicing teachers. The block of reading courses resulted in engaged teacher candidates because of the functional nature of the assignments that required knowledge of literacy learning and teaching theory as well as opportunities to plan and enact tutoring lessons for struggling literacy learners. According to Fang and Ashley, "The amount of quality reading gave students solid theoretical background on which they could draw to make sense of teaching and learning in the tutorial sessions" (p. 51).

Field experiences have an additional benefit for some teacher candidates. The vast majority of new teacher candidates come from European American ancestry and from middle class families. Some of these new teachers assume they will teach in the settings familiar to them—European American, middle class schools. Although the research has been mixed about this point, Groulx (2001) found that a field experience in an urban setting with students of minority backgrounds opened other teaching placement options for many teacher candidates. After a successful urban field experience, some teacher candidates decided to pursue teaching positions in urban school districts.

Although field experiences are generally beneficial, not all experience is educative (Dewey, 1938). Some field experiences socialize teacher candidates into the existing cultures of schools that are not successful. What can complicate this notion is that teacher candidates often view their field experiences as more valid and important than course work, even when particular school experiences might be deemed unproductive or detrimental (Toll, Nierstheimer, Lenski, & Kolloff, 2004). Therefore, field experiences need to be mediated by teacher educators with a wide range of perspectives as well as by professional course work that is grounded in research of best practices. This combination helps teacher candidates come to their own conclusions about the teaching methods that they will adopt as new teachers.

For example, Toll and her colleagues discussed a group of teacher candidates who were assigned to field experiences in a poor community with a large African American population. The teacher candidates observed primary-grade teachers who asked their students to complete page after page from workbooks. The young students were forced to sit in desks, often too small for them, for long stretches of time. The teachers did not use any of the literacy methods that the teacher candidates had learned in university classes, such as reading aloud to students, making words from word tiles, and explicitly teaching skills and strategies. When the teacher candidates returned to the university, they said that what they learned from their field experiences was that poor students did not have the background for the types of literacy ideas that they had learned but that they needed to use worksheets to "control" the class. The teacher candidates saw the students "as deficient in ways that were so strong as to require special instructional methods" (Groulx, 2001, p. 69). In this case, therefore, the teacher candidates learned a lesson that contradicted the practices they learned in their methods class. When these contradictions occur, teacher candidates need to make their own decisions about what to believe. Teacher preparation course work can assist teacher candidates in the decision-making process.

Meeting Students' Literacy Needs

As teacher candidates acquire knowledge about literacy teaching and learning and become adept at taking that theory into practice through field experiences, they still must keep their students' needs at the center of their instructional decision making. Leu and Kinzer (1999) support teachers' possessing enough knowledge about literacy to enable them to make minute-by-minute decisions based on students' changing and idiosyncratic needs and development, rather than relying on scripted materials or memorized methods. It is the classroom teacher who must know each student well enough to assess the individual literacy needs of his or her students and be able to respond in a way that is helpful and effective. "Only the classroom teacher who works with a child every day is in a position to know what is appropriate instruction for that particular child," writes Flippo (1998, p. 38). Dewey (1910/1991) echoes this stance when he discusses the need for teachers who are able to look at new situations and problems in a learning setting and be able to solve them in new and innovative ways. He believes that successful teachers are ones who act with flexibility and are able to always look toward future possibilities.

Conclusion

The Committee on Teacher Education (CTE), a division of the National Academy of Education, has sought to study research initiatives and provide research-based recommendations for teacher preparation curricula. As Cochran-Smith (2004) notes, the CTE posits that an agenda to improve and reform teacher preparation would include a movement toward professionalization. This agenda would strive to put teaching on a plane with professions such as law and medicine. It would involve establishing an official body of knowledge that "distinguishes professional educators from lay persons and ensures that teachers for all students are fully prepared and fully certified" (p. 114).

Teaching is a profession, such as medicine, whose course work is rigorous and steeped in research; therefore, one cannot imagine separating professional study from opportunities to practice. Darling-Hammond (2000) notes that teacher preparation and clinical experiences housed in professional settings can be purposefully and intentionally structured. She discusses the example of teaching hospitals that prepare medical professionals in the kinds of venues where they will be expected to function with excellence when their formal education is complete. Teacher preparation should not be a question of choosing either course work or field experiences; rather, combining course work and field experiences best prepares teaching professionals.

REFERENCES

Cochran-Smith, M. (2004). Ask a different question, get a different answer: The research base for teacher education. *Journal of Teacher Education, 55*(2), 111–115.

Cochran-Smith, M., & Lytle, S. (1999). Relationships of knowledge and practice: Teacher learning in communities. In A. Iran-Nejad & P.D. Pearson (Eds.), *Review of research in education* (Vol. 24, pp. 249–305). Washington, DC: American Educational Research Association.

Darling-Hammond, L. (1990). Teachers and teaching: Signs of a changing profession. In W.R. Houston (Ed.), *Handbook of research on teacher education* (pp. 267–290). New York: Macmillan.

Darling-Hammond, L. (2000). How teacher education matters. *Journal of Teacher Education, 51*(3), 166–173.

Dewey, J. (1938). *Experience and education*. New York: Macmillan.

Dewey, J. (1991). *How we think*. Buffalo, NY: Prometheus Books. (Original work published 1910)

Fang, Z., & Ashley, C. (2004). Preservice teachers' interpretations of a field-based reading block. *Journal of Teacher Education, 55*(1), 39–54.

Flippo, R.F. (1998). Points of agreement: A display of professional unity in our field. *The Reading Teacher, 52*, 30–40.

Goodfellow, J., & Sumsion, J. (2000). Transformative pathways: Field-based teacher educators' perceptions. *Journal of Education for Teaching, 26*(3), 245–257.

Groulx, J.G. (2001). Changing preservice teacher perceptions of minority schools. *Urban Education, 36*(1), 60–92.

Haberman, M.J. (1996). The preparation of teachers for a diverse free society. In L. Kaplan & R. Edelfelt (Eds.), *Teachers for the new millennium: Aligning teacher development, national goals, and high standards for all students* (pp. 127–130). Thousand Oaks, CA: Corwin Press.

International Reading Association. (2003). *Prepared to make a difference: Executive summary of the national commission on excellence in elementary teacher preparation for reading instruction.* Newark, DE: Author. Retrieved April 22, 2005, from http://www.reading.org/downloads/resources/1061teacher_ed_com_summary.pdf

Interstate New Teacher Assessment and Support Consortium. (1992). *Model standards for beginning teacher licensing and development: A resource for state dialogue* [Electronic version]. Washington, DC: Council of Chief State School Officers. Retrieved August 30, 2005, from http://www.ccsso.org/projects/interstate_new_teacher_assessment_and_support_consortium

Lenski, S.D., & Nierstheimer, S.L. (2004). *Becoming a teacher of reading: A developmental approach.* Upper Saddle River, NJ: Pearson/Merrill/Prentice Hall.

Leu, D., & Kinzer, C.K. (1999). *Effective literacy instruction, K–8* (4th ed.). Upper Saddle River, NJ: Merrill.

National Commission on Teaching and America's Future. (1996). *What matters most: Teaching for America's future.* Washington, DC: Author. Retrieved April 28, 2005, from http://www.zuni.k12.nm.us/ias/21te/nwrel/what.htm

Pearson, P.D. (2003). The role of professional knowledge in reading reform. *Language Arts, 81*(1), 14–15.

Shulman, L.S. (1986). Those who understand: Knowledge growth in teaching. *Educational Researcher, 15*(2), 4–14.

Toll, C.A., Nierstheimer, S.L., Lenski, S., & Kolloff, P.B. (2004). Washing our students clean: Internal conflicts in response to preservice teachers' beliefs and practices about literacy learning. *Journal of Teacher Education, 55*(2), 164–176.

Wise, A.E., & Leibbrand, J.A. (2000). Standards and teacher quality: Entering the new millennium. *Phi Delta Kappan, 81*(3), 612–616.

TRUTH 6

Teacher Preparation Programs Link Literacy Teaching With the Demands of Teaching in Schools

DEBRA K. WELLMAN AND LINDA S. WOLD

◆ ◆ ◆

In the 1950s, literacy methods courses were nonexistent and university-based teaching was insufficient to prepare future literacy teachers. Redesigned programs now provide more extensive field experiences that are structured to provide applications of current literacy research with best practices. To enhance teaching practice, field methods courses often are situated in elementary or secondary schools where on-site teaching provides opportunities for teacher candidates to learn firsthand from classroom teachers and to build more active, supportive learning communities.

Literacy professors in teacher preparation programs are expected to have expertise in the field of literacy as well as in methods of teaching. In many states, literacy teacher educators are required to split their time between the university and public schools where they also provide feedback and support to the interns in the field. The separate spaces for professors and classroom teachers have become blurred as the two have developed collaborative strategies to foster preservice teacher growth.

Professional partnerships between university faculty and classroom teachers provide a positive learning environment for preservice teachers to be able to connect what they learned in college courses to real classroom teaching opportunities. These professional partnerships provide for the exchange of knowledge and generate levels of expertise for each of the stakeholders.

◆ ◆ ◆

Literacy Teacher Preparation: Ten Truths Teacher Educators Need to Know by Susan Davis Lenski, Dana L. Grisham, and Linda S. Wold, Editors. Copyright © 2006 by the International Reading Association.

CHAPTER HIGHLIGHTS

◆ An increased number of literacy courses now provide teacher candidates with a breadth and depth of knowledge and experiences, although, in the United States, requirements vary by state.

◆ Integrated field experiences prepare teacher candidates to see the links between course work and teaching in schools.

◆ The collaborative nature of university and school partnerships fosters comprehensive improvements in teacher preparation and a seamless curriculum from theory to practice.

COLLABORATING ON TEACHER PREPARATION

The principal of Central Elementary School eagerly greets Professor Baker's reading diagnostic students on their first site visit. "We are proud to have a role in preparing future teachers, and we welcome you to Central Elementary School," he remarks. The teacher candidates listen intently to a brief introduction and engage in an interactive session about their new teaching site.

The principal continues, "It is our pleasure to have you here working side by side with veteran teachers. Each of you has been assigned to a specific teacher. As I call your name, please follow your cooperating teacher out of the media center, and your teacher will give you a quick tour of our school. After your tour, your teacher will take you to her classroom and introduce you to your students."

Professor Baker's teacher candidates work with small heterogeneous groups of students for the remainder of the semester. The course they are taking is designed to create a learning environment where they can implement a variety of diagnostic reading strategies that they learn in the college classroom. For example, at the beginning of the course, teacher candidates are taught the importance of understanding their students' interests. In order to link what they are learning in the diagnostic course, teacher candidates are required to give their small group of students a reading interest survey. As teacher candidates plan lessons throughout the semester, they can draw on the interests of their students to create individualized lessons.

At the close of the semester, the teacher candidates report learning valuable lessons beyond the content of the diagnostic course. By situating much of their course work in authentic classrooms, their cooperating teachers are able to provide feedback and encouragement on a variety of daily classroom situations.

The collaborative nature between literacy teacher educators and classroom teachers makes it possible for teacher candidates to begin to implement research-based best practices in literacy methods and to negotiate their roles as future literacy teachers. Such professional collaboration was not common practice in the past. However, redesigned teacher preparation programs have fostered connections to schools and have linked literacy methods teaching with the demands of teaching in schools.

Literacy Teaching as Research: The Balance of Theory and Practice

The tensions between educators adhering to theory and educators adhering to practical aspects of teaching are longstanding. In the 1950s, professors of literacy pioneered new methods to improve the teaching of literacy in elementary classrooms (Smith, 1986). Conflicts arose because many of the new ideas that were introduced into schools were purported to be more effective techniques but they had been created without contributions from classroom teachers. There were no field experiences required in teacher preparation programs to allow future teachers to apply the theory of literacy instruction with students in actual literacy classrooms. To strengthen teacher training in literacy, many teacher educators accepted the challenge to create explicit course work in literacy methods (Anderson, Hiebert, Scott, & Wilkinson, 1985).

Today, specific strategies for effectively teaching students how to read and write continue to be debated. The increased interest among teacher educators in conducting more research in authentic literacy classrooms has had strong implications for improved literacy instruction. For example, in their review of early literacy education research, Anders, Hoffman, and Duffy (2000) found four specific ways to improve the preparation of elementary literacy teachers:

1. additional and specific courses in literacy,

2. enhanced field and practicum experiences,

3. improved qualifications of teacher educators, and

4. collaborative efforts to improve teacher preparation programs.

Additional and Specific Courses in Literacy

Literacy teachers historically received little practical training in the teaching of literacy prior to working with students in their own classrooms. In the

1970s, many elementary literacy teachers were required to teach literacy with only one course in this area (Chall, 1975). According to Chall, this course was not sufficient to prepare teacher candidates for the demands of literacy instruction in elementary or secondary classrooms. For most teachers, the real training came through trial and error as they tried to teach literacy or from teachers' guides in basal book programs.

Shulman (1986) encourages more literacy course work so that "teacher candidates will teach effectively once they have acquired subject matter knowledge, become acquainted with models of innovative curriculum, and have practice using them" (p. 8). But Shulman also claims that future teachers need to deeply conceive of and integrate content knowledge with pedagogy to develop instructional practices that advance student learning. These were different goals to achieve in one course of literacy.

Today's elementary and secondary teacher candidates have a more comprehensive but varied preparation in literacy education. Some state licensing agencies leave the curriculum up to the individual colleges of education, while other states have begun to mandate specific courses in the training of literacy teachers. Because many teacher preparation programs strive to meet National Council for Accreditation of Teacher Education (NCATE) standards or state-approved programs for certification, there is more consistency in the preparation of teacher candidates. Even so, literacy teacher preparation courses are quite varied from program to program and are far from standardized (Anders et al., 2000).

What does appropriate teacher preparation in literacy look like? The amount of required literacy courses varies considerably. Flippo and Hayes (1984) surveyed state departments of education to find out if the requirements in literacy were similar for teacher certification. At that time, "they found a two-course requirement in 24 states, one course in 17 states, and 9 states leaving this decision to the local institutions" (p. 725). Twenty years later, many states require elementary education majors to take a minimum of four courses in literacy, and teacher candidates are required to have field experiences embedded in multiple content area methods courses. By the time teacher candidates are ready to begin student teaching, many have engaged in a broad range of clinical teaching experiences that were once reserved for student teaching.

Enhanced Field and Practicum Experiences

Universities and public schools have worked together to increase practicum experiences for future teachers. Although Feistritzer (1999) states that elementary and secondary education majors average 14 hours of clinical experiences to complete their teacher preparation program requirements, college and university programs meeting NCATE and state approval have a substantially greater number of required clinical hours. In fact, many teacher preparation programs situate their semester-long literacy methods courses in elementary schools to provide hands-on experiences during academic training. Prior to student teaching, required education courses generally provide teacher candidates with rich experiences in clinical settings in which teacher candidates work with students from a variety of grade levels and culturally diverse backgrounds. Therefore, quality literacy teacher preparation programs combine instruction with on-site field experiences that build an active learning community.

Literacy methods courses have been redesigned not only to provide teacher candidates with quality field experiences in literacy teaching but also to tap into the knowledge and expertise of classroom teachers. Teacher educators have become active participants in the placement process of teacher candidates and often model the teaching of literacy at field sites. The active role that teacher educators play in modeling best practices can begin to dampen the criticism that instructors are unaware of the realities of today's diverse public school literacy classrooms (Abdal-Haqq, 1998). As teacher educators continue to elicit support from elementary schools, the superb literacy teachers serve as positive role models to teacher candidates. Teacher candidates' observance and work in the presence of master literacy teachers also enhance collaborations between universities and elementary schools.

Quality literacy teacher preparation programs combine instruction with on-site field experiences that build an active learning community. These integrated field experiences "prepare better teachers by integrating pedagogical study with the practical realities of everyday classroom life" (McDermott, Gormley, Rothenberg, & Hammer, 1995, p. 184).

Improved Qualifications of Teacher Educators

Employment practices at colleges and universities show specific changes in the hiring of teacher educators, including certain required elementary or secondary teaching experiences and current teaching licenses. These new practices are intended to validate teacher educators' teaching expertise and affirm their ability to teach effectively. Current NCATE-accredited teacher preparation programs, as well as many state teacher certifying boards, also require university literacy methods course instructors to maintain a current teaching license and have three to five years of classroom teaching experience in the content areas they will teach to teacher candidates. Also, teachers certified by the National Board for Professional Teaching Standards (NBPTS) and content area experts are collaborating with teacher educators in exciting new ways. Many NBPTS-certified teachers are sought after to serve as adjunct faculty and to teach university courses to teacher candidates.

There may have been a time when teacher educators were inexperienced as classroom teachers, but that view changed with new accreditations and accountability for teacher preparation program faculty. It is unrealistic to assume that teacher educators lose sight of school reality when they exit elementary, middle, or secondary schools and enter college classrooms. In fact, because of the No Child Left Behind Act of 2001, teacher educators in literacy are being recruited to serve as literacy coaches or to provide seminars on current methods of teaching literacy and writing to all levels of teachers.

Master's degree programs in literacy education also are in high demand. Some states, in an effort to increase the number of highly qualified literacy teachers in classrooms, have established criteria for literacy endorsements. One way to prepare teachers who have had minimal courses in literacy in their undergraduate program is to encourage them to attend a quality master's degree program. In addition, as we write this chapter, interest in creating literacy coach positions in secondary education is widespread. Secondary teachers are now expected to teach reading skills as part of their content area instruction.

Collaborative Efforts to Improve Teacher Preparation Programs

Teacher educators understand that practicing teachers have a profound impact on the teacher candidates who are assigned to them during student teaching. Darling-Hammond (2003) has shown how the relationship between teacher candidates and mentors is most influential in regard to supporting the development of quality future teachers. The intention of such collaborative efforts is twofold: to build strong foundations between partner institutions, and to support the development of genuine relationships among teacher educators and elementary and secondary school faculty (Teitel, 2000).

Across the United States, many colleges and universities have created a stronger commitment to collaboration by creating Professional Development Schools (PDS) with regional schools. These collaborative efforts build reciprocal foundations between partner institutions. Teachers in the public schools become acquainted with the college faculty members and have opportunities to develop genuine working relationships with them. At the same time, college faculty members build important collegial relationships with practicing teachers to solidify efforts to improve the teaching skills of the teacher candidates placed in their care. Also, in PDS, public schools often benefit by recruiting new teachers from the pool of teacher candidates. Each partner contributes to the comprehensive process of training quality literacy teachers and benefits from active involvement through collaboration (Grisham, Laguardia, & Brink, 2000).

Teacher preparation in the 21st century is marked by stronger collaborations between teacher educators in literacy and classroom teachers. In PDS, the field experiences and the course work are more highly integrated for teacher candidates. In addition, cooperating teachers hold expertise and serve as mentors to these future teachers. Through valuable partnerships, universities and schools have increased collaboration and have engaged in mindful discussions of teacher preparation and pedagogy.

The intention of PDS is to show markedly improved learning for all students, classroom teachers, teacher educators, and teacher candidates (Teitel, 2000). Through dialogue among professors of literacy education and elementary teachers and principals, colleges of education have made changes in their programs, such as adding literacy courses to their offerings, to ensure that teacher candidates are prepared for future teaching. As McDermott and colleagues (1995) note, "Practical experiences, especially those in which novices receive extensive and varied classroom experiences and constructive evaluation about their teaching, help new teachers move more quickly to more mature thoughts about their teaching and children's learning" (p. 190).

Advancements in Literacy Teacher Preparation

Advancements in the preparation of literacy teachers have helped to dissolve the conflict between practicing teachers' perceptions and teacher educators' perceptions of what teacher candidates need to know to be successful literacy teachers. As one advancement, teacher educators and practicing teachers in elementary and secondary schools are seeking genuine collaboration to train future teachers. For example, Au and Valencia (1997) created a system of using curriculum standards and portfolio implementation to evaluate teacher candidate performances in literacy. Because both teachers and teacher educators were involved in the evaluation process, knowledge about the assessment process and teacher candidates' learning was enhanced by participation and extended professional development. Another example of a substantive change in literacy teacher preparation highlights how teacher educators in literacy link literacy methods course work to the *Standards for the English Language Arts* (International Reading Association & National Council of Teachers of English, 1996) to provide equal access to quality literacy teaching for all students in the United States. These important changes provide an initial research base for continued advancement in the preparation of literacy teachers, rather than perpetuating the lack of perspectives of literacy instruction that pervade the media. Because the foundational studies in literacy teacher preparation are still developing, it is clear that research needs to add to and build a stronger evidence base of support (Anders et al., 2000).

Conclusion

Over the past several decades, the training of literacy teachers in teacher preparation programs has transformed what literacy teachers know and are able to do to meet the needs of a diverse population of students. Specific changes have enhanced this training. This chapter has focused on the following improvements: quality course work and field experiences in elementary and secondary classrooms, improved qualifications of teacher educators, and collaborative developments between partner institutions. Such changes have affected how universities and schools work to solve concerns about literacy teacher preparation. The collaborative nature of university and school partnerships appears to be instrumental in addressing comprehensive improvements in teacher preparation (Teitel, 2000).

When considering what matters most in future improvements in teacher preparation, it is essential that researchers and practitioners continue to work together toward preparing more competent and qualified teachers. Collaboration requires envisioning a common goal in education. Shulman (1987) uses Fenstermacher's (1986) terms to explain these important goals, but Shulman explains that goals are not intended

> to indoctrinate or train teachers to behave in prescribed ways but to educate teachers to reason soundly about their teaching as well as to perform skillfully. Sound reasoning requires both a process of thinking about what they are doing and an adequate base of facts, principles, and experiences from which to reason. (p. 13)

Collaborative efforts between colleges of education and practicing teachers have helped to build a new teacher workforce. These new teachers are capable, well prepared, and eager to face the challenges of today's classrooms. This is a powerful reminder of strategic accomplishments in teacher preparation. Most important, these accomplishments should be acknowledged by U.S. policy analysts as teacher educators and teachers strive to create meaningful opportunities to advance how teachers learn to teach the world to read.

REFERENCES

Abdal-Haqq, I. (1998). *Professional development schools: Weighing the evidence.* Thousand Oaks, CA: Corwin Press.

Anders, P.L., Hoffman, J.V., & Duffy, G.G. (2000). Teaching teachers to teach reading: Paradigm shifts, persistent problems, and challenges. In M.L. Kamil, P.D. Pearson, P.B. Mosenthal, & R. Barr (Eds.), *Handbook of reading research* (Vol. 3, pp. 719–742). Mahwah, NJ: Erlbaum.

Anderson, R., Hiebert, E.H., Scott, J., & Wilkinson, I. (1985). *Becoming a nation of readers: The report of the Commission on Reading.* Washington, DC: The National Institute of Education.

Au, K.H., & Valencia, S.W. (1997). The complexities of portfolio assessment. In D.T. Hansen & N.C. Burbules (Eds.), *Teaching and its predicaments* (pp. 123–144). Boulder, CO: Westview.

Chall, J. (1975). The reading problem: A diagnosis of the national reading problem; a national strategy for attacking the reading problem; legislative and administrative actions. In J. Caroll (Ed.), *Toward a literate society: The report of the Committee on Reading of the National Academy of Education* (pp. 3–45). New York: The National Academy.

Darling-Hammond, L. (2003). Keeping good teachers: Why it matters, what leaders can do. *Education Leadership, 60*(8), 6–13.

Feistritzer, C.E. (1999). *The making of a teacher: A report on teacher preparation in the U.S.* Washington, DC: National Center for Education Reform. Retrieved April 22, 2005, from http://www.edutopia.org/php/resources.php?id=item_216595

Fenstermacher, G.D. (1986). Philosophy of research on teaching: Three aspects. In M.C. Wittrock (Ed.), *Handbook of research on teaching* (3rd ed., pp. 37–49). New York: Macmillan.

Flippo, R.F., & Hayes, D.A. (1984). *Preparation in reading and educator certification: Requirements, needs, issues.* Boone, NC: American Reading Forum and Appalachian State University. Retrieved April 22, 2005, from http://www.americanreadingforum.org/84_yearbook/%20 pdf/10_flippo.pdf

Grisham, D.L., Laguardia, A., & Brink, B. (2000). Partners in professionalism: Creating quality field experience for teacher candidates. *Action in Teacher Education, 21*(4), 27–40.

International Reading Association & National Council of Teachers of English. (1996). *Standards for the English language arts.* Newark, DE; Urbana, IL: Authors.

McDermott, P., Gormley, K., Rothenberg, J., & Hammer, J. (1995). The influence of classroom practical experiences on student teachers' thoughts about teaching. *Journal of Teacher Education, 46*(3), 184–191.

No Child Left Behind Act of 2001, Pub. L. No. 107-110, 115 Stat. 1425 (2002).

Shulman, L.S. (1986). Those who understand: Knowledge growth in teaching. *Educational Researcher, 15*(2), 4–14.

Shulman, L.S. (1987). Knowledge of teaching: Foundations of the new reform. *Harvard Educational Review, 57*(1), 1–22.

Smith, N.B. (1986). *American reading instruction.* Newark, DE: International Reading Association. (Original work published 1934)

Teitel, L. (with Abdal-Haqq, I.). (2000). *Assessing the impacts of professional development schools.* Washington, DC: American Association of Colleges for Teacher Education Publications.

Teacher Preparation Programs Situate School Curricula in the Larger Context of Teaching and Learning

MARVA CAPPELLO AND NANCY FARNAN

◆ ◆ ◆

As teacher candidates build conceptual ideas about teaching, they learn to situate instruction in the context of theoretical, practical, and instructional knowledge. A teacher candidate's goal is to teach transferable skills that will allow him or her to provide multiple applications for student learning, opportunities for responsive instruction, and the tools to meet the needs of all student learners, including the culturally and linguistically diverse richness that populates our literacy classrooms. Because there is no one best way to teach literacy effectively, teacher candidates must learn to choose the highest quality programs that also provide the greatest learning potential. They do this by learning about local school curricula and how those curricula foster literacy learning. Literacy teacher preparation requires that teacher candidates learn to both implement best practices based on research and evidence and implement school curricula. Teacher candidates also make instructional decisions as they negotiate national, state, and local accountability measures. Professional development schools and other strong university–school collaborations are effective organizational structures for providing exemplary preparation experiences. Best practices are targeted in national standards to enable teacher candidates to determine what students know and are able to do.

◆ ◆ ◆

Literacy Teacher Preparation: Ten Truths Teacher Educators Need to Know by Susan Davis Lenski, Dana L.
Grisham, and Linda S. Wold, Editors. Copyright © 2006 by the International Reading Association.

CHAPTER HIGHLIGHTS

◆ Teacher candidates must be equipped with transferable skills for multiple applications for all students.

◆ National and state agencies have brought a new degree of conformity to teacher preparation programs.

◆ Teacher preparation programs have become more regulated by national and state accountability measures as a result of stricter accreditation processes.

◆ Teacher preparation programs teach the curricula used in schools.

◆ Teacher candidates are able to move between different curricula and literacy programs because of their knowledge of literacy principles.

◆ Professional development schools and other strong university–school collaborations foster enhanced student learning and exemplary teacher preparation experiences.

BROAD-BASED LITERACY KNOWLEDGE

I [Marva Cappello] first observed Jody's work with third-grade students at an urban elementary school that serves a diverse student population. Over several visits, I watched her teach a required literacy unit. The many objectives for the unit include distinguishing fantasy from reality, developing vocabulary, and identifying parts of speech from the school's adopted literacy textbook. Jody worked from a well-organized plan that centered on the grade-level standards and her grade-level team's agreements for technology, all well within the teaching standards and expectations required and regulated by U.S. and state accountability measures. When asked what knowledge or experiences she had drawn upon in her planning, Jody replied that she was able to plan effectively and work well with colleagues because she had the fundamental understanding of critical theories associated with teaching language arts and she clearly understood what the team members were trying to accomplish in the language arts curriculum and through their instruction. In addition, Jody expressed a strong knowledge of a wide range of strategies, such as concept mapping, graphic organizers, and writing through the curriculum, which she could adapt to any program or teaching situation:

> By the time I got to my student teaching placement, I was familiar with the programs from the experiences in our methods classes and from our textbook. I looked at the standards first, then the story, and then I decided which strategies to use with the text activities suggested. There was too much to do in the program to do everything in it. I used the program to guide my decisions about how to meet the standards.

Critics often are quick to claim incompatibility between a university's teacher preparation programs and the curricula of schools served by new teachers (Burstein, Kretschmer, Smith, & Gudoski, 1999). In fact, some critics view new teachers as so underprepared that the curricula must act like and do the work of a teacher (Troen & Boles, 2003). In recent times, the dialogue has intensified, with teacher preparation seen as the culprit responsible for K–12 students' failure to achieve desired levels in literacy and mathematics (Cochran-Smith, 2003), and part of that sense of culpability comes from the claim that new teachers do not teach what students in these schools are required to learn. The evidence, however, suggests something quite different. That is, teacher preparation programs are highly regulated enterprises that must meet rigorous standards to become accredited in the states in which they operate. In short, teacher preparation programs do prepare teacher candidates to teach the curricula used in schools.

Evidence indicates that teacher candidates, such as Jody, and newly credentialed teachers are well prepared to face schools' pedagogical and programmatic requirements as they plan to teach the curriculum and meet the needs of their students. Teacher educators support teaching the curriculum used in schools, and when specific curricular programs are examined in various teacher preparation courses, they are situated in the larger context of concepts related to teaching and learning.

Teacher preparation programs align their goals to school curricula in a variety of ways. For example, a particular literacy program's emphasis on teaching phonics would be placed in the larger context of theories and research related to learning to read and the pedagogical circumstances involved in that process. Another example is when university faculty teach theories of first- and second-language acquisition during teacher preparation so that new teachers are informed regarding how linguistically diverse children and adolescents develop language proficiency. Research on how best to help students develop language proficiency directly informs instruction, such as using Specially Designed Academic Instruction in English Strategies (e.g., graphic organizers and Total Physical Response). As a result, new teachers with this repository of theoretical, research-based, and instructional knowledge can confidently implement curricula within specific programs and plan instruction designed to ensure success for a diverse student population. With this knowledge, new teachers can make informed decisions and create optimal circumstances for teaching content to ensure all students an equal opportunity for learning.

Beyond School Curricula

The history of education reform movements over the past several decades illustrates why it is important for teacher preparation institutions to provide teacher candidates with an array of effective pedagogical processes and, in addition, to present critical curriculum considerations in the various disciplinary and skill areas (Klausmeier, 1990). Interstate New Teacher Assessment and Support Consortium (INTASC; 1992) states,

> INTASC believes that all education policy should be driven by what we want our P–12 students to know and be able to do. Thus, all aspects of a state's education system should be aligned with and organized to achieve the state's policy as embodied in its P–12 student standards—this includes its teacher licensing system. (n.p.)

Teacher candidates must know how to teach culturally and linguistically diverse learners; use various assessment processes and understand the relation between assessment and instruction; ensure that students effectively can read various texts with a variety of text structures; choose an appropriate curriculum and design instruction so all students develop effective reading comprehension skills; and effectively use multiple forms of communication such as oral language, writing, and technological literacy. All of these critical elements are required for licensure of teacher credential programs and are explicitly stated in teacher credentialing standards across the United States. Included in the study of curriculum and instruction are various curricular programs, rather than one program, taught in schools. The responsibilities of teacher preparation institutions are to provide instruction that helps teacher candidates know the programs of highest quality and to ensure that teacher candidates have the skills and dispositions to evaluate the various programs to begin their development of professional judgment.

Responsive Instruction in Teacher Preparation Programs

Complementing the highly planned curriculum of university literacy methods courses are the voices of student teachers. As teacher candidates visit schools and engage in professional conversations in schools, they bring questions about specific adopted programs back to university classrooms, where discussions center on how the programs implement the various curricular and instructional elements that teacher candidates have learned. As a result, teacher candidates are provided with theoretical grounding and strategic tools that can be appropriated for any teaching situation. In other words, the goal of the university is not a commercial one; it is to teach transferable skills.

Why is this transfer important and even necessary? Teacher candidates may be hired for teaching positions in a number of contexts other than that in which they student teach and engage in field experiences. For example, the county we serve has 42 public school districts and 590 public schools that use a variety of the state-approved literacy materials. In addition, individual school districts implement programs differently. Some school districts opt to require teachers to follow scripts rigidly, while others use specific program materials to support language arts learning across the curriculum. Our county also is home to many private and charter schools, each with unique pedagogical foci. There is no one program dominating our county. Indeed, schools adopt and implement programs in many different ways. Also, many teacher candidates choose for various reasons to leave the locality where they were trained, including to return home, to move to an entirely new locale, or to relocate because of a dearth of teaching positions in the area.

What program should teacher preparation courses emphasize? Even if all public and private schools in a particular locale decided to universally adopt one literacy program, teacher preparation institutions would be doing teacher candidates and the students they teach a grave disservice. The National Reading Panel report (National Institute of Child Health and Human Development, 2000) and other research reports have made it clear that there is no one right way to teach literacy and that teachers should know multiple ways to be effective. There can be no universal approach to literacy curriculum and materials (Allington & Walmsley, 1995).

Therefore, teacher preparation programs have the complex job of providing teacher candidates with a theoretical grounding that supports literacy methods and strategies, as well as attempting to familiarize them with various types of programs and with programs currently in use, and helping them develop evaluative skills to judge new programs and curricula as school districts consider adopting them. All of this is regulated by multiple systems on a variety of levels.

National Accountability

U.S. teacher preparation institutions are held accountable for their programs by national regulatory agencies such as the National Council for Accreditation of Teacher Education (NCATE) and INTASC. These agencies ensure that institutions meet agreed-upon standards that represent the latest research on producing effective novice teachers. NCATE is a coalition of 35 professional associations of teachers, teacher educators, content specialists, and local and state policymakers representing over 3 million individuals, all committed to quality teaching. The U.S. Department of Education and the Council for Higher Education Accreditation recognize NCATE as a professional accrediting body for teacher preparation (NCATE, 2005).

Regarding the content knowledge required of teachers, in its evaluation of teacher preparation programs, NCATE (2002) requires that "accredited schools, colleges, and departments of education should ensure that new teachers attain the necessary content, pedagogical, and professional knowledge and skills to teach both independently and collaboratively" and that "teacher candidates know the subject matter that they plan to teach and can explain important principles and concepts delineated in professional, state, and institutional standards" (p. 3). This is similar to INTASC's policy statement mentioned earlier in this chapter (see p. 67). Clearly, national accreditation agencies expect states' curriculum and content standards to be an integral part of teacher candidates' knowledge base.

In addition, NCATE (2002) standards "promote increased university and school partnerships in the design and implementation of clinical experiences" (n.p.). Again, it is evident that the expectation in the preparation of teachers is for strong collaboration between teacher preparation and P–12 schools, specifically that they share resources and expertise. Teacher preparation programs are evaluated by NCATE on their integration of experiences and knowledge to reach shared understandings, including in the critical areas of curriculum and instructional processes.

State-Level Accountability

Each state in the United States has its own accrediting agency for teacher preparation programs, and each state's requirements are different; however, there are underlying commonalities and requirements. In 2002–2003, the faculty from the College of Education at San Diego State University, San Diego, California, undertook an examination of teacher preparation standards across the United States. We highlight here a few of the findings from that effort.

Colorado states the connection of teacher preparation programs with schools' curricula explicitly in Standard Three, which the state adopted in January 2000:

> Standard Three: Knowledge of Standards and Assessment. The teacher shall be knowledgeable about strategies, planning practices, assessment techniques, and

appropriate accommodations to ensure student learning in a standards-based curriculum.

The teacher has demonstrated the ability to:

3.1 Design short- and long-range standards-based instructional plans.

3.5 Use assessment data as a basis for standards-based instruction.

3.8 Ensure that instruction is consistent with school district priorities and goals, the Colorado Model Content Standards, and the 1999 Colorado Accreditation Program. (Colorado Department of Education, 2000, n.p.)

The state of Florida states this connection a little differently but just as explicitly in their administrative rules, "Essential Practices: Planning." One of Florida's key indicators of "accomplished practice" is that teachers are able to work "with various education professionals, parents, and other stakeholders in the continuous improvement of the educational experiences of students" (Florida Department of Education, 2003, n.p.).

California has yet another way of expressing its commitment to a connection between K–12 schools and teacher preparation programs. In its Standard 5: Effective Curriculum, Teaching, and Assessment Practices, the California Commission on Teacher Credentialing (CCTC; 2001) states that "elements of this standard address the curriculum, instruction, and assessment practices of the California State Curriculum Frameworks and Standards within each subject area for which these documents have been adopted" (n.p.). In California, teacher preparation is highly regulated through a number of agencies and accountability measures. The CCTC is an active agency that has established California Standards for the Teaching Profession and, more recently, Teaching Performance Expectations (TPEs) that all teacher candidates must meet to earn their credentials. The standards and expectations that center on literacy are rigorous and also very clear. For example, Domain 1 under Content Specifications in Reading, Language, and Literature states that "candidates...are able to identify and demonstrate an understanding of the fundamental components of human language, including phonology, morphology, syntax, and semantics, as well as the role of pragmatics in using language to communicate" (CCTC, 2001 n.p.). In Appendix A of the document, the CCTC is clear when it states, according to Education Code Section 44259 (b)(5), that "the commission shall ensure that subject matter standards and examinations are aligned with the state content standards and performance standards adopted for pupils pursuant to subdivision (a) of Section 60605" (n.p.). (Note: Section 60605 lists reading, writing, mathematics, history–social science, and science.)

California's TPE #1A specifically addresses the subject of curriculum in two ways. First, the CCTC (2001) expects teacher candidates to be able to go beyond adopted literacy programs, requiring that "[teacher candidates] understand how to use instructional materials that include a range of textual, functional, and recreational texts and how to teach high quality literature and expository text" (n.p.). In addition, TPE #1A requires that "candidates for a Multiple Subject Teaching Credential demonstrate the ability to teach the state-adopted academic content standards for students in English-Language Arts (K–8)" (n.p.). In fact, the credentialing agency requires that new teachers have a command of the California Student Academic Content Standards and State Curriculum Frameworks, not only for literacy but also for all of the content areas. The CCTC also makes explicit the strong link between standards and the literacy curriculum:

> Each candidate participates in intensive instruction in reading and language arts methods that is grounded in methodologically sound research and includes exposure to *well-designed instructional programs*, which enable candidates to provide a comprehensive, systematic program of instruction that is aligned with the California state-adopted academic content standard. (n.p.)

In addition to the California Standards for the Teaching Profession and TPEs, the CCTC requires that teacher candidates pass the Reading Instruction Competence Assessment (RICA) to earn credentials. The RICA is a large-scale test that addresses content specifications within four instructional domains:

> The purpose of the RICA is to ensure that candidates for Multiple Subject Teaching credentials...possess the knowledge and skills important for the provision of effective reading instruction to students. The goal of reading instruction is to develop competent, thoughtful readers who are able to deliver effective reading instruction that is based on the results of ongoing assessment; that reflects knowledge of state and local reading standards for different grade levels; that represents a balanced, comprehensive reading curriculum; and that is sensitive to the needs of all students. (CCTC, 2001, p. 1)

School-Level Accountability

Many K–12 schools set their own schoolwide goals that include and go beyond the state's content standards. For example, to promote schoolwide literacy, every student in one Florida middle school reads *The Giver* (Lowry, 1993) during an academic year. There also may be grade-level agreements for instruction that are specific to a particular school. For example, while Jody, the student teacher from the opening vignette, was juggling the demands of meeting California's TPEs and the California Content Standards across the third-grade curriculum and preparing to pass the RICA examination, during her preservice year she also satisfied the third-grade team's agreement to use available technology to teach students to create a brochure or newsletter. Jody integrated this supplemental project into a unit found in the school's adopted literacy textbook. Other schools may ask teachers to negotiate a schoolwide focus (such as expository writing or English-language development) while meeting state and national standards.

Teacher preparation programs across the United States are licensed to prepare new teachers to meet on many levels the demands of the profession, schools, and communities. Classroom teachers teach and assess content standards; adapt curricula and instruction to meet the needs of culturally and linguistically diverse students; work with parents and the community to provide for the psychological, social, and emotional needs of students; and do much more. Teacher preparation standards both across the United States and within individual states address, monitor, and evaluate these areas of skills, dispositions, and knowledge.

What Is Working in Teacher Preparation Programs

In 2004, the California State University (CSU) system published results of the 2003 CSU *Systemwide Evaluation of Professional Teacher Preparation Programs: An Initiative of the California State University Deans of Education* (2003), a survey conducted with teacher preparation programs on 22 CSU campuses. Surveys were sent to 10,622 teacher preparation program graduates and student teaching supervisors by using a stratified random sample.

The survey results indicate a high level of perceived preparedness in many areas by both the graduates and their employment supervisors, including new teachers' ability to work with the curricula found in schools. Supervisors reported that 89% of new teachers from both Multiple and Single Subject Programs were well prepared "to know and understand the subjects of the curriculum at his or her grade level(s)" (CSU, 2003, p. 30). Ninety-one percent of graduates from Single Subject Programs were evaluated by supervisors to be "well or adequately prepared" to "teach [his or her] primary subject according to State Academic Content Standards," and 89% were evaluated as prepared to "use textbooks and other materials aligned with State Content Standards" (p. 43). Regarding preparedness in the area of literacy, graduates from Multiple Subject Programs were evaluated by 83% of supervisors as "well or adequately prepared" to "teach reading-language arts according to California Standards in Reading" (p. 41). Across all content areas, the highest evaluation by supervisors of new teachers' preparation to teach schools' curricula was 84% in literacy and mathematics.

This ambitious survey highlights strengths as well as areas where additional work is needed systemwide to ensure teacher candidates' ability to, among other things, teach the curricula used in schools. The CSU survey results clearly show that teacher preparation programs in California teach teacher candidates about the curricula used in schools and seem to do it most expertly in literacy and mathematics. We think it is important to note that the CSU Deans of Education are the driving force behind this survey, which is now in its second year of being conducted for the purpose of analyzing, evaluating, and continually reviewing program strengths to ensure the preparation of exemplary new teachers.

Professional Development Schools

At many universities, teacher preparation cohort groups are developed with the theories of professional development schools (PDS) in mind. The PDS are organizational structures in which schools and universities converge in an effort to unite the theoretical and the practical. NCATE (2002) has developed and adopted—as of March 2001—program standards for PDS and explicitly describes their organizational structure and purpose:

> Professional development schools are innovative institutions formed through partnerships between professional education programs and P–12 schools. Their mission is professional preparation of candidates, faculty development, inquiry directed at the improvement of practice, and enhanced student learning. (n.p.)

Strong PDS and other school–university collaborations involve the stakeholders in meaningful partnerships for the purpose of providing exemplary teacher preparation experiences. Literature on PDS is abundant (see, for example, Abdal-Haqq, 1998; Grisham et al., 1999), and there has long been awareness that the structures and reward systems of the K–12 schools and the university are different (Labaree, 1999). Recent evaluations of school–university partnerships reveal that teacher candidates who are prepared within such collaborations have better retention rates and are better prepared for teaching (Darling-Hammond, 2003). In PDS and other school–university collaborations, field experiences and course work are integrated to a high degree. Schools are the recipients of certain kinds of expertise and the mentors of new teachers. University work is theory grounded in practice, and teacher educators are both mentors to teacher candidates and recipients of expertise (Ash, 2003).

PDS represent the epitome of relevance in teacher preparation. Although PDS can be highly problematic in terms of time and effort, given that these collaborations often depend upon the concerted efforts of dedicated individuals—often without rewards or sufficient resources—they provide for collaboration between professional teacher preparation programs and the schools in which teacher candidates are being prepared to teach.

Conclusion

Teacher preparation programs are highly regulated enterprises that must meet rigorous standards to become accredited in the states in which they reside. Teacher preparation course work at its best teaches about the programs that local schools use and situates those programs within a curricular framework that emphasizes best practices in teaching for student learning. The role of teacher educators is to teach teacher candidates to use principles of effective teaching (Brophy, 1999) as guidelines for reviewing materials, making decisions about student needs that align with research-based practices, and targeting lessons for optimal learning. Brophy (1999) recommends that classroom teachers align curricula with specific principles that include learning to evaluate curricula coherently in different content areas, help students solve problems across different subjects, and teach for meaning and learning transfer. The end result of such foundational structures suggests that teacher candidates will be able to think broadly and critically about effective curriculum implementation.

Teacher preparation programs do much more than prepare teacher candidates to implement one specific curricular program because a teacher preparation program's goals are not commercial. Because teacher candidates may find teaching positions outside the localities where they complete their student teaching assignments, new teachers need to know how to make informed decisions about what is best for their students based on a variety of factors, including available materials and considerations of students' cultural, linguistic, and community backgrounds.

REFERENCES

Abdal-Haqq, I. (1998). *Professional development schools: Weighing the evidence.* Thousand Oaks, CA: Corwin Press.

Allington, R.L., & Walmsley, S.A. (Eds.). (1995). *No quick fix: Rethinking literacy programs in America's elementary schools.* New York: Teachers College Press.

Ash, G.E. (2003, December). *Progress as potential: The evaluation of a long-term literacy professional development program for middle school teachers.* Paper presented at the 53rd Annual Meeting of the National Reading Conference, Chicago, IL.

Brophy, J. (1999). *Teaching. Educational practices—1.* Geneva, Switzerland: International Bureau of Education.

Burstein, N., Kretschmer, D., Smith, C., & Gudoski, P. (1999). Redesigning teacher education as a shared responsibility of schools and universities. *Journal of Teacher Education, 50*(2), 106–118.

California Commission on Teacher Credentialing (CCTC). (2001). *Standards of program quality and effectiveness professional teacher preparation programs.* Retrieved June 5, 2005, from http://www.csupomona.edu/~ls/adopted%20ms%20standards.pdf

California State University (CSU). (2003). *Systemwide evaluation of professional teacher preparation programs: An initiative of the CSU deans of education.* Long Beach, CA: Office of the Chancellor.

Cochran-Smith, M. (2003, December). *Promises and politics: Images of research in the discourse of teaching and teacher education.* Paper presented at the 53rd Annual Meeting of the National Reading Conference, Chicago, IL.

Colorado Department of Education. (2000). *Performance-based standards for Colorado teachers.* Retrieved June 6, 2005, from http://www.cde.state.co.us/cdeprof/li_perfbasedstandards.htm

Darling-Hammond, L. (2003). Keeping good teachers: Why it matters, what leaders can do. *Education Leadership, 60*(8), 6–13.

Florida Department of Education. (2003). *State board of education, administrative rules.* Retrieved June 7, 2005, from http://www.firn.edu/doe/rules/6a-5.htm

Grisham, D.L., Bergeron, B., Brink, B., Farnan, N., Lenski, S.D., & Meyerson, M.J. (1999). Connecting communities of practice through professional development school activities. *Journal of Teacher Education, 50*(3), 182–191.

Interstate New Teacher Assessment and Support Consortium (INTASC). (1992). *Model standards for beginning teacher licensing and development: A resource for state dialogue* [Electronic version]. Washington, DC: Council of Chief State School Officers. Retrieved August 30, 2005, from http://www.ccsso.org/projects/interstate_new_teacher_assessment_and_support_consortium

Klausmeier, R.L. (1990). Four decades of calls for reform of teacher education: The 1950s through the 1980s. *Teacher Education Quarterly, 17*(4), 23–64.

Labaree, D.F. (1999). Too easy a target: The trouble with ed schools and the implications for the university. *Academe, 85*(1), 34–39.

National Council for Accreditation of Teacher Education (NCATE). (2002). *Professional standards for the accreditation of schools, colleges, and departments of education.* Retrieved June 6, 2005, from http://www.ncate.org/public/standards.asp?ch=4

National Council for Accreditation of Teacher Education (NCATE). (2005). *About NCATE.* Retrieved June 6, 2005, from http://www.ncate.org/public/aboutNCATE.asp

National Institute of Child Health and Human Development (NICHD). (2000). *Report of the National Reading Panel. Teaching children to read: An evidence-based assessment of the scientific research literature on reading and its implications for reading instruction* (NIH Publication No. 00-4769). Washington, DC: U.S. Government Printing Office.

Troen, V., & Boles, K.C. (2003). *Who's teaching your children?: Why the teacher crisis is worse than you think and what can be done about it.* New Haven, CT: Yale University Press.

LITERATURE CITED

Lowry, L. (1993). *The giver.* New York: Houghton Mifflin.

TRUTH

Traditional Teacher Preparation Programs Better Prepare Future Literacy Teachers Than Do Alternative Routes

BETTE S. BERGERON

◆ ◆ ◆

Alternative route teacher preparation refers to the methods of preparing teachers, not to their credentialing. Although the terms alternative route *and* alternative certification *often are used interchangeably, this chapter uses them in distinct ways:* alternative route *refers to the methods of preparing teachers and* alternative certification *defines the credentialing of teacher candidates (Allen, 2003).*

Can alternative providers offer programs of comparable quality to universities? Can nontraditional providers produce literacy teachers of the same quality and caliber as traditional teacher preparation programs? Or are these suppositions only myths that are promoted by those who are distrustful of traditional teacher preparation programs and the universities in which they reside? As examined through the research, we suggest that the "truth" lies in the quality of traditional teacher preparation and the potential for success for those classroom literacy teachers who complete quality teacher preparation programs.

◆ ◆ ◆

CHAPTER HIGHLIGHTS

◆ Quality teacher preparation makes a difference for teachers and their students.

◆ There is a strong relationship between student achievement and a teacher's preparation.

◆ School administrators rate traditionally prepared teachers higher in terms of instructional competence and quality of instruction as compared with alternative route teachers.

◆ Great disparity exists between the quality and components of alternative route programs and that of traditional programs.

◆ While their overall effectiveness is questioned, alternative route programs have been successful in attracting nontraditional candidates into the profession.

◆ *All* teacher preparation programs must guarantee that every student benefits from a highly qualified literacy teacher.

◆ Ultimately, better prepared teachers are more successful than those who are less prepared.

A VIEW OF ALTERNATIVE TEACHER PREPARATION

Jim, a university program coordinator, is not supportive of "fast-track" teacher preparation. He states,

> I truly believe a quality preservice education program must include time for reflection. However, our unit has to try to formulate something because our competitors are active in offering accelerated options. As a consequence, we are starting a fast-track [12-month] program for postbaccalaureate students. Despite our efforts, many students are washed out due to the rapid nature and stress in learning to become a teacher in one year.

When asked if there are any successes with this program, Jim notes,

> One success story of alternative certification is Sharon, who started as a classroom volunteer, moved into an internship, completed her student teaching, and then landed her first job, all in the same school. I occasionally run into Sharon, and she appears to be successful and enjoys teaching. That is not the case with others in our alterative program, however. We have numerous quitters, whiners, and complainers. The cohort has altercations with school administration, faculty, and even amongst themselves. Teachers have to know so much. Asking them to learn it in an abbreviated time is not fair to them or to the students they will be teaching.

The dilemma about how best to prepare quality literacy teachers is riddled with uncertainty and questions, particularly for teacher educators who are working diligently to improve the effectiveness of literacy instruction in teacher preparation. At the heart of the controversy are the questions, "How is *quality* being defined in teacher preparation?" and "Does the quality of teacher preparation make a difference in teacher candidates' effectiveness in teaching?"

Preparing Quality Literacy Teachers

Although research on teacher preparation is replete with research specific to quality teacher preparation in general, much less information has been reported on the preparation of quality *literacy* teachers. Dillon (D. Dillon, personal communication, June 15, 2004), noted literacy educator, describes the preparation of highly qualified literacy teachers as being a complex and multifaceted process:

> It is acknowledged in the research literature that a strong knowledge base is key to a literacy teacher's success: Teachers need to understand how children's literacy abilities are nurtured; the role of texts, tasks, and purposes for reading and writing on children's development; the role of assessment and evaluation in fostering quality teaching and learning experiences; the development of a motivating and literate environment; and the role of professional development across a teacher's career. However, the literature is also clear that knowledge alone is not enough to prepare and sustain effective teachers. Quality literacy teacher preparation includes multiple and varied opportunities to apply new knowledge and skills under the guidance of quality mentors who provide constructive feedback and coaching. What is clear is that quality teacher preparation in literacy takes time, money, and expertise: There is important content to be learned and connected to form a coherent vision of, and basis for, good teaching.

In 2003, the International Reading Association (IRA) released a report regarding the preparation of excellent literacy teachers in the United States. The commission charged with this task selected eight exemplary teacher preparation programs and identified the following characteristics:

- *content*—a comprehensive curriculum;
- *apprenticeship*—a variety of course-related field experiences;
- *vision*—programs centered around a vision of literacy and quality teaching;
- *resources and mission*—sufficient resources to support quality preparation;

- *personalized teaching*—responsive teaching and an adapted curriculum;
- *autonomy*—institutional advocacy to ensure that students receive a quality experience;
- *community*—an active learning community that is developed with faculty, students, and mentor teachers; and
- *assessment*—continual evaluation of students, the program, and alumni to guide future program development (IRA, 2003).

Content knowledge and field experiences are particularly critical in identifying exemplary programs for literacy teachers (Harmon et al., 2001). The programs identified as exemplary by IRA's Excellence in Reading Teacher Preparation Commission offered content that included theoretical foundations, sound instructional practices, the means for assessing students' literacy progress, and accommodations for diverse learners. Content also was aligned with professional reading standards. The Commission identified carefully monitored field experiences as being a critical program feature when they are embedded in authentic classroom instruction over extended periods of time and in collaboration with expert classroom teachers.

The Commission conducted a comparative three-year study of the effectiveness of graduates from the eight exemplary programs in terms of classroom practices and student achievement. During their first year in the classroom, graduates from quality programs were responsive to students, had extensive knowledge of the reading process, and implemented a variety of assessment strategies (Maloch, Fine, & Flint, 2002/2003). The results of this study found that well-prepared teachers are more successful and confident than other beginning teachers and are more effective in creating literacy-rich classroom environments that engage students in reading. Perhaps most compelling is that students of the exemplary graduates have higher gains in reading achievement (IRA, 2003). From these studies, we can conclude that quality teacher preparation makes a difference in the professional lives of literacy teachers and in the academic potential of their students.

Findings on Traditional Literacy Teacher Preparation

Research indicates that quality literacy teacher preparation does make a difference for teachers and their students (see Table 8.1 for resources that show the advantages of both kinds of teacher preparation). These differences relate to the quality and evaluation of the teacher candidates' preparation.

TABLE 8.1
Resources on the Advantages of Traditional and Alternative Route (AR) Programs

	Advantage of Traditional Program	Advantage of AR Program
Attraction of diverse teacher candidates		Finn, C.E., & Madigan, K. (2001). Removing the barriers for teacher candidates. *Educational Leadership, 58*(8), 29–31, 36. Haberman, M. (2004). *Alternative certification: Intended and unintended consequence.* Retrieved May 28, 2004, from http://www.teach-now.org/frmNews_SanAntonio2004.asp Laczko-Kerr, I., & Berliner, D.C. (2003). In harm's way: How undercertified teachers hurt their students. *Educational Leadership, 60*(8), 34–39. Resta, V., Huling, L., & Rainwater, N. (2001). Preparing second-career teachers. *Educational Leadership, 58*(8), 60–63. Wilson, S.M., Floden, R.E., & Ferrini-Mundy, J. (2002). Teacher preparation research: An insider's view from the outside. *Journal of Teacher Education, 53*(3), 190–204.
Quality of teacher candidates	Keller, B., & Galley, M. (2002, June 19). *Paige uses report as a rallying cry to fix teacher ed.* Retrieved June 12, 2004, from http://www.edweek.org/ew/newstory.cfm?slug=41title2.h21	Archibald, G. (2003, July 16). *Federal education report finds shortage of qualified teachers* [Electronic version]. Washington, DC: The Washington Times. Retrieved June 12, 2004, from www.washingtontimes.com/functions/print.php?StoryID=20030715-114915-3853r
Teaching performance	Darling-Hammond, L., & Youngs, P. (2002). Defining "highly qualified teachers": What does "scientifically-based research" actually tell us? *Educational Researcher, 31*(9), 13–25. Hoffman, J., & Pearson, P.D. (2000). Reading teacher education in the next millennium: What your grandmother's teacher didn't know that your granddaughter's teacher should. *Reading Research Quarterly, 35*(1), 28–44. Laczko-Kerr, I., & Berliner, D.C. (2003). In harm's way: How undercertified teachers hurt their students. *Educational Leadership, 60*(8), 34–39.	

	Advantage of Traditional Program	Advantage of AR Program
Student achievement	Darling-Hammond. L. (2001b). *The right to learn: A blueprint for creating schools that work*. San Francisco: Jossey-Bass Darling-Hammond, L., & Youngs, P. (2002). Defining "highly qualified teachers": What does "scientifically-based research" actually tell us? *Educational Researcher, 31*(9). 13–25. Hoffman, J., & Pearson, P.D. (2000). Reading teacher education in the next millennium: What your grandmother's teacher didn't know that your granddaughter's teacher should. *Reading Research Quarterly, 35*(1). 28–44. Laczko-Kerr, I., & Berliner, D.C. (2003). In harm's way: How undercertified teachers hurt their students. *Educational Leadership, 60*(8), 34–39. Tell, C. (2001). Making room for alternative routes. *Educational Leadership, 58*(8), 38–41.	
Responsiveness to student needs	Maloch, B., Fine, J., & Flint, A.S. (2002/2003). "I just feel like I'm ready": Exploring the influence of quality teacher preparation on beginning teachers. *The Reading Teacher, 56*, 348–350.	
Knowledge of pedagogy	Berry, B. (2001). No shortcuts to preparing good teachers. *Educational Leadership, 58*(8), 32–36. Laczko-Kerr, I., & Berliner, D.C. (2003). In harm's way: How undercertified teachers hurt their students. *Educational Leadership, 60*(8), 34–39. Littleton, M., Beach, D., Larmer, B., & Calahan, A. (1991). An effective university-based alternative certification program: The essential components. *Teacher Education and Practice, 7*(1), 37–43. Maloch, B., Fine, J., & Flint, A.S. (2002/2003). "I just feel like I'm ready": Exploring the influence of quality teacher preparation on beginning teachers. *The Reading Teacher, 56*, 348–350.	

(continued)

TABLE 8.1 (continued)
Resources on the Advantages of Traditional and AR Programs

	Advantage of Traditional Program	Advantage of AR Program
Teacher retention	Darling-Hammond. L. (2001b). *The right to learn: A blueprint for creating schools that work.* San Francisco: Jossey-Bass. Darling-Hammond. L., & Youngs, P. (2002). Defining "highly qualified teachers": What does "scientifically-based research" actually tell us? *Educational Researcher, 3*1(9), 13–25. Laczko-Kerr, I., & Berliner, D.C. (2003). In harm's way: How undercertified teachers hurt their students. *Educational Leadership, 60*(8), 34–39.	
Teacher candidates' perceptions of their own teacher preparations and the teaching profession	Darling-Hammond. L. (2001b). *The right to learn: A blueprint for creating schools that work.* San Francisco: Jossey-Bass. Darling-Hammond. L., & Youngs, P. (2002). Defining "highly qualified teachers": What does "scientifically-based research" actually tell us? *Educational Researcher, 3*1(9), 13–25. Hoffman. J., & Pearson. P.D. (2000). Reading teacher education in the next millennium: What your grandmother's teacher didn't know that your granddaughter's teacher should. *Reading Research Quarterly, 35*(1). 28–44. Laczko-Kerr, I., & Berliner, D.C. (2003). In harm's way: How undercertified teachers hurt their students. *Educational Leadership, 60*(8), 34–39. Wilson, S.M., Floden, R.E., & Ferrini-Mundy, J. (2002). Teacher preparation research: An insider's view from the outside. *Journal of Teacher Education, 53*(3). 190–204.	
Administrators' perceptions of teacher candidates	Darling-Hammond. L. (2001b). *The right to learn: A blueprint for creating schools that work.* San Francisco: Jossey-Bass. Darling-Hammond. L., & Youngs, P. (2002). Defining "highly qualified teachers": What does "scientifically-based research" actually tell us? *Educational Researcher, 3*1(9), 13–25.	

Intensive teacher preparation, quality university-based course work, and field experiences provide multiple opportunities for teacher candidates to learn and apply the knowledge of their profession. When large-scale studies are examined, a strong relation is found between student performance and an individual teacher's preparation (Darling-Hammond & Youngs, 2002); also important is whether or not the teacher is fully certified. When contrasted with Alternative Route (AR) teacher candidates, traditionally prepared teachers have a broader view of curriculum, more clearly understand student ability and motivation, and more effectively translate content into practice (Laczko-Kerr & Berliner, 2003). They also are more positive about staying in the profession (Wilson, Floden, & Ferri-Mundy, 2002). Most important, students with teachers who are fully prepared learn more than students whose teachers have little or no traditional teacher preparation (Darling-Hammond, 2001b; Laczko-Kerr & Berliner, 2003).

The evaluation of traditionally prepared teachers is also quite positive. For example, administrators rate teacher candidates from traditional programs higher than those in AR programs on instructional skills and planning. When compared to teachers who are trained alternatively, traditionally prepared teachers also rate their own teacher preparation programs higher (Darling-Hammond, 2001b), have a lower dropout rate in both their training and teaching, and have more self-confidence (Laczko-Kerr & Berliner, 2003). The research literature also links measures of teacher expertise and teacher preparation to student achievement (Darling-Hammond & Youngs, 2002) and quality teaching.

Defining Quality Alternative Routes to Teaching

In her recent state-by-state analysis, Feistritzer (2004) defines true AR programs as those designed for attracting talented, nontraditional individuals into teaching, and she reports that more than 200,000 teachers have been licensed through AR programs. One of the strengths of AR programs is indeed their success in attracting potential candidates who are nontraditional in terms of diversity in age, ethnicity, and prior work experience. Initially, AR programs broadened the pool of teachers to fill critical shortages and created a more representative demographic population of teachers (Wilson et al., 2002). Rudenga (E. Rudenga, personal communication, June 15, 2004), a literacy educator, supports graduates of AR programs who are prepared through focused and quality programs:

We have found that those seeking an accelerated, alternative certification come with rich life experiences, which have created a knowledge base that allows them to discern effective literacy strategies. Others have worked in the classroom and have observed students learn to read and know of both the struggles and successes. Because these future teachers have firsthand experiences, they are able to both understand and translate literacy theory into practice. I expect the next generation of teachers, who enroll in accelerated, alternative programs, will bring a depth of experience, understanding, and knowledge that form a solid base for future learning and implementation of literacy strategies.

Rudenga's description is relevant to many teacher preparation programs, which are working to develop quality AR programs. However, because AR programs are variable and often the responsibility of local schools, the term is hard to define or compare. The definitions of AR programs show that design and quality vary within and across states (Darling-Hammond & Youngs, 2002). Although some AR programs provide very limited teacher preparation before entry into the classroom, others require extensive course work, professional development, and mentoring support for novices in their first year of teaching. For the purposes of this chapter, however, AR programs are defined as those that limit the amount of pedagogical knowledge presented to teacher candidates before they assume full-time classroom responsibilities and accelerate the teacher preparation process.

Issues Related to Alternative Route Programs and Literacy Teacher Preparation

Research on the impact of AR programs is limited and offers decidedly mixed findings (Wilson et al., 2002) that are exaggerated by a lack of consensus regarding definitions and features of AR programs. On the positive side, compared to traditional teacher preparation programs, AR programs do appear to more successfully attract nontraditional and minority teachers into the classroom. Many midcareer adults bring maturity and life experience to the profession and have both depth and breadth of content knowledge (Resta, Huling, & Rainwater, 2001). However, the following issues contribute to the debate on AR programs:

- inconsistencies in AR program course work,
- varied practice teaching experiences among AR programs, and
- the effect of AR programs on education policy.

Inconsistencies in AR program course work. The course work that is required by AR programs is inconsistent from program to program. AR course work largely is nonstandardized and based on individual institutional programs and state standards (Darling-Hammond, 2001a). Program requirements range from no course work to hundreds of clock hours of university-based instruction. This inconsistency presents issues that concern teacher educators as well as literacy teachers who must teach side by side with diversely prepared peers. Darling-Hammond (2001b) notes that "crash courses in teaching" (p. 15) generally fail and observes that most teachers who are alternatively trained leave the profession by their third year. Berry (2001) finds that shortcut programs often thrust under prepared teachers into the most challenging classrooms and devalue the knowledge and skills demanded by the profession today.

Under Reading First legislation (part of the No Child Left Behind Act of 2001), teachers are required to use "scientifically based" methods that focus on five defined elements of reading instruction. A Reading First Network has been established to engage teacher preparation programs in the realignment of reading instruction with defined research-based practices (Hertz, 2003). This requirement should provide better course alignment within AR programs.

Varied practice teaching experiences among AR programs. The methods of teaching in elementary and secondary schools vary according to institutional and state requirements. Yet some AR programs, such as Teach for America (TFA), provide minimal classroom teacher preparation and teaching apprenticeships. Tell (2001) argues that highly accelerated programs such as TFA fail to train teachers adequately, and she questions the policy of placing the least experienced teachers in those schools where students need the best instruction. In an interview by Scherer (2001), Berliner also remarked that TFA candidates have had extreme difficulties because they simply have not had the training needed to teach in the settings in which they are placed. Darling-Hammond (1994) also found that TFA graduates fare much worse than graduates from other AR programs. TFA recruits have high attrition rates; produce students who perform much lower than traditionally prepared teachers on math, literacy, and language arts tests; feel markedly less well prepared than graduates of traditional teacher preparation programs; and question their abilities to meet students' individual instructional needs (Darling-Hammond & Youngs, 2002).

Although teacher preparation programs need to incorporate strategic field experiences, neither the quality nor the duration have been mandated.

Consequently, the application of research theory into practice is largely weakened and unevenly applied in AR programs.

The effect of AR programs on education policy. Although a national focus on education issues can lead to improvements in professional practices, it also can polarize the debate on quality in teacher preparation in the United States. Former U.S. Secretary of Education Rod Paige published a report titled *Meeting the Highly Qualified Teachers Challenge: The Secretary's Second Annual Report on Teacher Quality* (2003). In the report, Paige proposes that AR programs attract academically stronger recruits who persist in the profession at a higher rate than those who are traditionally prepared, and he argues that traditional teacher preparation is not producing enough quality teachers. He urges states to revamp their teacher certification requirements by setting higher standards for content knowledge, while requiring less teacher preparation in teaching methods for AR and Alternative Certification (AC) programs (Keller & Galley, 2002). Darling-Hammond and Youngs (2002) argue that the report refers to unscientific newspaper articles and documents, which may have the effect of bolstering the case for tougher academic content tests and AC (Keller & Galley, 2002). To provide clarification, IRA's Board of Directors issued a policy statement urging that literacy teachers participate in an open dialogue with policymakers, while continuing to inform the public of the impact of legislation on schools (IRA, 2000).

Positive Findings of the Research on Alternative Route Programs

The research indicates that streamlined teacher preparation programs often "produce recruits who consider themselves underprepared, are viewed as less competent by principals, are less effective with students, and have high rates of teacher attrition" (Darling-Hammond & Youngs, 2002, p. 23). Research findings on AR programs are not always negative, however. Some state data indicate that teachers who have graduated from AR programs have higher retention rates than those from traditional programs (Feistritzer, 2004). The presence of intense classroom instruction, on-the-job training, and the support of college faculty and teachers contribute to higher retention. Feistritzer also suggests that AR programs increase the representation of minorities in the United States' teaching force.

Haberman (2004) suggests that AR programs have put extraordinary pressure on traditional university-based programs to become more accountable for their graduates. He reports additional findings that show

how AR programs have caused widespread change in teacher preparation by demonstrating that

- content knowledge is the primary knowledge base teachers need,

- teaching know-how and methods are best learned on the job, and

- hiring a critical mass of teachers from AR programs can turn around failing schools.

Despite the enthusiasm shared by some policymakers regarding ARs to teacher preparation, however, the issue of quality supersedes the programs' conveniences and purported advantages. Berliner (personal communication, June 14, 2004), a university scholar involved in longstanding teacher preparation research, shares his concerns:

> Short alternative programs, especially those that provide few or no teaching methods courses and that also fail to provide extensive student teaching experiences, do *not* send to schools teachers who can efficiently learn to teach on the job. At a minimum those beginning teachers are missing an understanding of the big ideas of their disciplines, which are needed to teach, and they are missing the concepts and pedagogical techniques for organizing and managing their classrooms effectively. This is why they leave teaching rapidly, compared to those who come to teaching through more traditional routes. Furthermore, alternatively prepared teachers of the type described above do harm. Research suggests that such teachers provide students one month *less* academic growth than do teachers who come from more traditional programs. It is of course possible to design alternative programs that help new teachers to thrive and do little harm. But we should be very suspicious of alternative teacher training programs that are deficient in methods courses and fail to provide lengthy, supervised student teaching experiences.

Alignment of Traditional Teacher Preparation and Alternative Route Programs

Although research clearly shows the ineffectiveness of many aspects of AR programs as compared to traditional teacher preparation programs, accelerated teacher preparation programs have emerged in part to address a very real crisis—the United States' teacher shortages. How can the teaching profession better meet the demands caused by this crisis while assuring that all candidates are prepared in quality programs?

When AR programs are carefully constructed, the research suggests that the differences are minimized between graduates of these programs and

TABLE 8.2
Resources on the Components of Quality AR Programs

Berry, B. (2001). No shortcuts to preparing good teachers. *Educational Leadership, 58*(8), 32–36.

Darling-Hammond, L. (2001b). *The right to learn: A blueprint for creating schools that work.* San Francisco: Jossey-Bass.

Littleton, M., Beach, D., Larmer, B., & Calahan, A. (1991). An effective university-based alternative certification program: The essential components. *Teacher Education and Practice, 7*(1), 37–43.

Miller, J.W., McKenna, B.A., & McKenna, M.C. (1998). A comparison of alternatively and traditionally prepared teachers. *Journal of Teacher Education, 49*(3), 165–176.

Resta, V., Huling, L., & Rainwater, N. (2001). Preparing second-career teachers. *Educational Leadership, 58*(8), 60–63.

Wilson, S.M., Floden, R.E., & Ferrini-Mundy, J. (2002). Teacher preparation research: An insider's view from the outside. *Journal of Teacher Education, 53*(3), 190–204.

graduates of traditional teacher preparation programs. In a study by Miller, McKenna, and McKenna (1998), graduates of a traditional teacher preparation program were compared with those who completed an AR program that included condensed course work, an induction-mentoring program, and ongoing course work to meet minimal state certification guidelines. After three years, there appeared to be no observable differences between the groups in teaching behavior, student output, or graduates' perceptions of their own competence. These researchers suggest that AR programs can be successful when they are designed to include mentoring, postgraduation training, inservice classes, and ongoing university supervision.

Research also suggests that carefully constructed AR programs produce teachers who are more effective than teachers who complete an AR program with less training and support (Darling-Hammond & Youngs, 2002). High-quality AR programs must demand that teacher candidates meet the same high standards as recruits of traditional teacher training programs (Darling-Hammond, 2001b). The research on quality AR programs points to the following critical features (see Table 8.2 for resources on the components of quality AR programs):

- high entrance standards for and rigorous screening of teacher candidates;

- extensive mentoring and supervision of teacher candidates;

- training of mentor teachers;

- extensive pedagogical teacher preparation in instruction, management, and curriculum;

- frequent evaluation of teacher candidates;
- practice for teacher candidates in lesson planning and implementation prior to assuming full-time teaching responsibilities; and
- high exit standards for teacher candidates.

Conclusion

Overall, the research appears to indicate that traditionally prepared teachers and their students tend to be more successful than alternatively prepared teachers and their students. As teacher shortages continue to pervade the education landscape, those who prepare future teachers must continue to find ways to balance issues of quality and quantity. Littleton, Beach, Larmer, and Calahan (1991) found that it is incumbent upon universities to offer quality AR programs, specifically for nontraditional teacher candidates. Teacher preparation programs cannot address their critics or the United States' teacher shortages without these considerations. The challenge is in creating teacher preparation programs that guarantee that every student benefits from a teacher—and specifically a literacy teacher—who is truly "highly qualified."

The examination of issues related to the teacher preparation of quality literacy teachers shows that, because of critical teacher shortages and political pressure, many institutions are developing AR programs that often accelerate the teacher preparation process while streamlining—or eliminating—pedagogical training. Although these routes often attract mature adults and minority teacher candidates, most research finds that these underprepared teachers academically disadvantage their students and struggle with issues related to lesson accommodation and assessment. It is unfortunate that these teachers too often leave the profession at a very high rate.

Because they attract the rich diversity of nontraditional students and offer working adults the opportunity to pursue careers in the classroom, AR programs do have an important role in teacher preparation when they provide quality alternatives and quality teacher preparation.

Does quality teacher preparation really make a difference in the lives of teachers and their students? Research strongly supports the idea that those teachers who are better prepared ultimately are more successful than those who are not. However, although much is known about the impact of quality teacher preparation overall, it is also important that teacher educators continue to conduct research on how best to prepare literacy teachers (Hoffman & Pearson, 2000). IRA is continuing to study teacher preparation so accurate information about the nature and impact of quality literacy teacher preparation programs ensures that there is a quality literacy teacher in every student's classroom.

The author wishes to thank Elizabeth Hinde and Stephanie Robertson for their assistance in the preparation of this chapter.

REFERENCES

Allen, M.B. (2003). *Eight questions on teacher preparation: What does the research say?* Denver, CO: Education Commission of the States.

Berry, B. (2001). No shortcuts to preparing good teachers. *Educational Leadership, 58*(8), 32–36.

Darling-Hammond, L. (1994). Who will speak for the children? How "Teach for America" hurts urban schools and students. *Phi Delta Kappan, 76*(1), 21–34.

Darling-Hammond, L. (2001a). The challenge of staffing our schools. *Educational Leadership, 58*(8), 12–17.

Darling-Hammond, L. (2001b). *The right to learn: A blueprint for creating schools that work.* San Francisco: Jossey-Bass.

Darling-Hammond, L., & Youngs, P. (2002). Defining "highly qualified teachers": What does "scientifically-based research" actually tell us? *Educational Researcher, 31*(9), 13–25.

Feistritzer, C.E. (2004). *Alternative teacher certification: A state-by-state analysis.* Retrieved April 22, 2005, from http://www.teach-now.org/frmintroduction.asp

Haberman, M. (2004). *Alternative certification: Intended and unintended consequence.* Retrieved May 28, 2004, from http://www.teach-now.org/frmNews_SanAntonio2004.asp

Harmon, J., Hedrick, W., Martinez, M., Perez, B., Keehn, S., Fine, J.C., et al. (2001). Features of excellence of reading teacher preparation programs. In J.V. Hoffman, D.L. Schallert, C.M. Fairbanks, J. Worthy, & B. Maloch (Eds.), *Fiftieth yearbook of the National Reading Conference* (pp. 262–274). Chicago: National Reading Conference.

Hertz, C. (2003, September 15). Paige announces $4.5 million grant to enhance teacher preparation in reading at minority-serving institutions. Retrieved April 25, 2005, from http://www.ed.gov/news/pressreleases/2003/09/09152003.html

Hoffman, J., & Pearson, P.D. (2000). Reading teacher education in the next millennium: What your grandmother's teacher didn't know that your granddaughter's teacher should. *Reading Research Quarterly, 35*(1), 28–44.

International Reading Association (IRA). (2000). *On U.S. government policy on the teaching of reading.* Retrieved April 25, 2005, from http://www.reading.org/resources/issues/positions_us_government.html

International Reading Association (IRA). (2003). *Prepared to make a difference: An executive summary of the National Commission on Excellence in Elementary Teacher Preparation for Reading Instruction.* Newark, DE: Author. Retrieved July 11, 2005, from http://www.reading.org/downloads/resources/1061teacher_ed_com_summary.pdf

Keller, B., & Galley, M. (2002, June 19). Paige uses report as a rallying cry to fix teacher ed. Retrieved June 12, 2004, from http://www.edweek.org/ew/newstory.cfm?slug=41title2.h21

Laczko-Kerr, I., & Berliner, D.C. (2003). In harm's way: How undercertified teachers hurt their students. *Educational Leadership, 60*(8), 34–39.

Littleton, M., Beach, D., Larmer, B., & Calahan, A. (1991). An effective university-based alternative certification program: The essential components. *Teacher Education and Practice, 7*(1), 37–43.

Maloch, B., Fine, J., & Flint, A.S. (2002/2003). "I just feel like I'm ready": Exploring the influence of quality teacher preparation on beginning teachers. *The Reading Teacher, 56,* 348–350.

Miller, J.W., McKenna, B.A., & McKenna, M.C. (1998). A comparison of alternatively and traditionally prepared teachers. *Journal of Teacher Education, 49*(3), 165–176.

No Child Left Behind Act of 2001, Pub. L. No. 107-110, 115 Stat. 1425 (2002), Part B, Subpart I, Sec. 1201-1208. Retrieved June 2, 2005, from http://www.ed.gov/policy/elsec/leg/esea02/pg4.html

Paige, R. (2003). *Meeting the highly qualified teachers challenge: The secretary's second annual report on teacher quality.* Jessup, MD: U.S. Department of Education.

Resta, V., Huling, L., & Rainwater, N. (2001). Preparing second-career teachers. *Educational Leadership, 58*(8), 60–63.

Scherer, M. (2001). Improving the quality of the teaching force: A conversation with David Berliner. *Educational Leadership, 58*(8), 6–10.

Tell, C. (2001). Making room for alternative routes. *Educational Leadership, 58*(8), 38–41.

Wilson, S.M., Floden, R.E., & Ferrini-Mundy, J. (2002). Teacher preparation research: An insider's view from the outside. *Journal of Teacher Education, 53*(3), 190–204.

Assessment Has a Dual Purpose in Teacher Preparation Programs

THOMAS P. CRUMPLER AND ELLEN SPYCHER

◆ ◆ ◆

Teacher preparation programs use assessment as a way to gauge teacher candidates' knowledge of pedagogy and practice. Therefore, excellent teacher preparation programs use multiple measures to assess teacher candidates. Assessments are then used to make informed literacy program decisions and to augment practices that have a positive impact on the effectiveness of literacy instruction. Teacher preparation programs also instruct teacher candidates on methods of assessing K–12 students' literacy practices inside and outside of schools. The duality of assessment, then, becomes apparent as we assess the knowledge of our teacher candidates, while at the same time model best pedagogical practice for them as they prepare for work in the profession.

While teacher educators assess the knowledge of the teacher candidate on one level, the candidate must also continually monitor his or her performance as he or she reflects and revises his or her practices to demonstrate effectiveness in multiple areas of literacy instruction. In a review of literacy research, the National Reading Panel (NRP) report of 2000 (National Institute of Child Health and Human Development) determined that teacher candidates need to know and be able to teach phonemic awareness, phonics, vocabulary, fluency, and comprehension, and they must be able to demonstrate successful performance when teaching these important aspects of literacy instruction. According to the accreditation standards of the National Council for Accreditation of Teacher Education (1999), more than half of all U.S. teacher preparation programs use performance-based assessment to evaluate the quality of teacher preparation. As a key part of preparing future teachers, literacy curricula involves planning, implementation, and reflection-based literacy practices that target the NRP goals and also other strategic areas of preparation, such as writing and special needs assessments.

◆ ◆ ◆

CHAPTER HIGHLIGHTS

◆ Assessment is characteristic of strong literacy teacher preparation programs.

◆ A teacher preparation program's assessment supports the development of teacher candidates' knowledge, skills, and dispositions when it is systematic, linked to classroom experiences, performance based, and mediated by constructive feedback.

◆ Excellent literacy teacher preparation programs use assessment of teacher candidates to affect teacher quality.

USING INFORMAL ASSESSMENT WITH STUDENTS

Claire, a senior elementary education major, expresses that she felt prepared to utilize her knowledge of assessment when she was faced with the opportunity in a classroom setting. She states,

> On the very first day of my field experiences, my cooperating teacher placed me with a guided literacy group. I noticed that a little girl was struggling and was not able to keep up with the rest of the group. After a conference with my cooperating teacher, I asked if I could reevaluate the student. I did several informal assessments with her and found that she had been placed in an inappropriate literacy group. With the permission of my cooperating teacher, I moved the student into a group that was more appropriate for her. I quickly noticed that she was doing quite well and enjoying her reading a bit more. My cooperating teacher was impressed with my ability to assess a student, and I was pleased to be able to put some of my undergraduate training to work in a real school setting.

A ssessment of students' literacy progress is an important component of a teacher's work. In literacy teacher preparation programs, teacher candidates learn to use their knowledge of assessment to determine students' literacy needs. Teacher preparation programs must ensure that teacher candidates are able to make instructional decisions using a variety of assessments. One way to accomplish this goal is to provide teacher candidates with performance assessments of their own learning. A second method is to have teacher candidates assess a student's literacy learning and make instructional recommendations to the classroom teacher, as in the opening vignette. Both aspects of assessment are important in the continuing development of teacher candidates.

Research on Assessment of Literacy Teachers

Teaching is a complex activity that necessitates the mastery of both subject knowledge and pedagogical knowledge, and, consequently, a systematic assessment that measures both knowledge types is needed (Davis & Sumara, 1997). Often, it seems that teacher candidates are assessed either on content knowledge with standardized tests or pedagogical knowledge through observation by supervisors with checklists outlining teaching behaviors. Separating these two domains of effective teaching for assessment efficiency diminishes the opportunity to capture the complex organization and implementation of both types of knowledge. A systematic assessment that aligns more closely with what teaching literacy actually entails provides better data about how subject and pedagogical knowledge are marshaled in quality teaching. Literacy is conceptualized as a meaning-making process in which knowledge of phonemic awareness, phonics, vocabulary, fluency, and comprehension all must be orchestrated successfully (Block, Gambrell, & Pressley, 2002; National Institute of Child Health and Human Development, 2000). As students progress through the grades, demands in content area literacy increase, and the other essential components for vocabulary, fluency, and literacy comprehension remain critical to and interrelated for successful readers (Snow, Burns, & Griffin, 1998; Stanovich, 2000). Assessing teacher candidates in ways that allow them to demonstrate their understanding of this development is vital in the preparation of highly qualified teachers.

Effective literacy teachers cannot rely on a preset list of strategies when working with diverse learners in today's schools. In reality, effective literacy teachers make decisions, access resources, and deliver instruction using research-based practices that are tailored to the needs and goals of individual learners. Teacher preparation programs that educate teacher candidates to orchestrate instructional decisions need to develop performance assessments that both assess the teacher candidates now and provide a sound background for them to use in the future (Pearson, Destefano, & Garcia, 1998).

Assessments of teacher candidates should measure such things as higher order thinking skills. For example, if in a lesson students do not understand how to implement a certain strategy that focuses on comprehension skills, a teacher candidate can ascertain this effectively and then make a decision about refocusing teaching at that point, rather than plodding through the rest of the lesson. Or, if students are involved in discussion about a work of literature that expresses a variety of views or interpretations, a teacher candidate's ability to summarize and synthesize ideas while still honoring students' diverse opinions is important for creating a strong learning community in that classroom. Assessments of teacher candidates should evaluate this type of thinking that is critical for successful teaching. Such assessments often rely on human judgment in scoring and require careful attention to issues of validity (Linn & Baker, 1996). Validity refers to an assessment's ability to successfully measure what it is supposed to measure. Assessments that capture curricular and procedural knowledge and predict a candidate's potential for successful teaching must involve more than a multiple-choice test. Minimally, such an assessment must be performance based—candidates must construct a response or demonstrate some aspects of teaching. Ensuring an acceptable level of validity for this type of assessment requires training or professional development for those doing the assessing.

Involving stakeholders in this type of assessment (e.g., practicing teachers, teacher educators, and the candidates themselves) could be an aspect of what has been called a "culture of learning" (Shepard, 2000, p. 13). Shepard's work has suggested that performance assessment should be about promoting a culture in which assessment is viewed as opportunities for dialogue among teacher candidates, practicing teachers, and teacher educators. When assessment of teacher candidates is situated within a larger culture of learning, assessment can be reconceptualized as promoting teacher growth and achievement. This reconceptualization shifts the purposes of assessment of teacher candidates toward both identifying exemplary teaching practices and encouraging professional development. Such a shift would help link educating and assessing teacher candidates in ways that are more valid than current assessments.

The Contested Terrain of Teacher Candidate and Program Assessment

In a historical perspective, assessment of teacher candidates' literacy knowledge has not been a high priority for researchers in the field (Anders, Hoffman, & Duffy, 2000). Although this trend is changing, there are not yet studies that provide detailed evidence regarding the best practices for assessment of teacher candidates or the programs that educate them. This situation is further complicated by the emphasis by school districts and the federal government on teacher candidate performance and K–12 achievement data for both assessment and accountability (Darling-Hammond, 2000). The result is that teacher educators who are committed to educating high-quality literacy teachers need to look carefully and thoughtfully at how to link the shift toward performance assessment in teacher preparation programs with the increase in evaluating K–12 schools on the basis of achievement data.

The current state of program assessment of teacher candidates is contested in the sense that there is ample evidence that reform is needed but there is no clear, agreed-upon direction for that change (Allen, 2003). Future reform efforts very likely will require teacher preparation programs to partner with school districts to craft experiences that will meet the needs of both the programs and the districts, thereby graduating well-prepared, highly qualified teachers.

Assessment of Teacher Candidates

Assessing teacher candidates' knowledge of theory and practice is part of the foundation of teacher preparation because such assessments help teacher preparation programs evaluate the competencies of their graduates and, in turn, their own success. These assessments are especially salient for programs because they strive to prepare teacher candidates to be successful. Teacher educators must welcome assessment as central to helping teacher candidates understand the challenges of teaching literacy to all students. Often, assessments of teacher candidates' knowledge of literacy has been administered only at the end of the teacher candidates' preparation. This view of assessment ignores the concept of development that is key to teacher candidates' understanding of literacy. A program's assessment of teacher candidates' knowledge and skills as a literacy teacher should be developed using the following two guidelines:

1. Assessment of teacher candidates should be systematic and linked closely to actual classroom experiences.

2. Assessment of teacher candidates should be performance based and provide them with feedback in a real setting.

Assessment in teacher preparation programs should have a purpose and a logical design, and it should assess or measure what it claims to measure. For example, if an assessment's purpose is to best gauge a teacher candidate's ability to diagnose a third-grade student's literacy comprehension skills, a multiple-choice test would not be the best choice. As a more logical form of assessment, the teacher candidate would need to observe and listen to a student actually reading in an instructional setting, evaluate that reading event with sound research-based criteria, write a description of that student's skills, and suggest instructional options for the student.

The assessment of a teacher candidate is performance based because the teacher candidate demonstrates the ability to construct and carry out a lesson, receive constructive feedback, and reflect on the process afterward. This assessment occurs formally during the teacher candidate's field experiences, and it also takes place less formally as the teacher candidate is observed during student teaching.

A Model of Systematic Performance-Based Assessment

The type of assessment that could best capture the complexity of teacher candidates' curricular and pedagogical knowledge as well as their knowledge of best practices is a performance-based assessment. Performance-based assessment, as found in college or university teacher preparation programs, should be a three-part process that involves planning instruction, implementing instruction while being observed, and reflecting on the process.

An example of a performance-based assessment task is when a teacher candidate is assigned to work with one student for a period of time during one semester. With the guidance of a teacher educator, the teacher candidate is responsible for assessing the student's strengths and needs and for planning and implementing instruction. During the performance-based assessment phase, the teacher candidate first plans a lesson based on a variety of informal assessments (e.g., inventories, running records, and miscue analysis). In this planning phase, the teacher candidate must clarify the strengths and needs of the student and use this information to plan a lesson. This planning must take into consideration best-practice instruction as well as whatever is known about the student, such as interests or special needs.

The second phase of the performance-based assessment involves the actual implementation of the lesson. The teacher candidate provides a complete written lesson plan to the teacher educator prior to the beginning of the lesson. The teacher candidate then teaches the lesson as the teacher educator observes. At the completion of the lesson, the teacher educator sits with the teacher candidate and offers immediate feedback.

The third and final phase of the performance-based assessment involves the teacher candidate writing a thorough reflection about the lesson. This reflection provides an opportunity for the teacher candidate to evaluate him- or herself in terms of what is successful, what is problematic, and what could or should be changed in the future. Reflection is not merely thinking about the sequence of the plan; rather, the goal of reflection is to encourage the teacher candidate to think deeply about the instructional goals, the response and learning of the student, and their potential links to larger learning goals.

Another assessment used in a literacy course with teacher candidates is the portfolio. During the semester in which the teacher candidate works directly with a learner, the teacher candidate is required to submit a portfolio chronicling his or her experiences. The portfolio is a compilation of the semester's work and includes a profile of the learner, all assessments used during the tutoring experience, plans for instruction based on the strengths and needs of the student, lesson plans, and a detailed plan for future literacy instruction. This portfolio also is a performance-based assessment because it provides an opportunity for teacher candidates to review and assemble assignments from the semester and reflect on this compilation as evidence of their growth. Further, it serves as a means of assessing the understanding of the teacher candidates as they plan and implement instruction.

This sequence of performance-based assessment does not capture all aspects of a candidate's development of instructional competency and understanding of literacy. However, within this sequence, there is a place for progressive refinement of the content knowledge and pedagogical knowledge exhibited by a candidate. In addition, this multiple-phased assessment can also be refined by teacher educators based on working with the candidates, reviewing the results of the performance assessments, and using those results to examine reliability of this sequence. Such an approach affords a much more comprehensive view of the complex work of teaching.

Performance-Based Assessment and the Value of Partnerships

The assessment of teacher candidates in teacher preparation programs is not straightforward; rather, it is multifaceted and best addressed on a variety of levels. These levels include assessment of the teacher candidate's knowledge as well as what he or she is able to accomplish in the classroom. Tension forms when teacher preparation programs use performance-based assessment with teacher candidates who enter schools that use primarily standardized tests to assess student learning. How can teacher preparation programs link performance-based assessments of teacher candidates with K–12 achievement data that is salient to public schools? One answer to this question draws on some of Darling-Hammond's (1997) scholarship on educational reform and work by some of our Australian colleagues on literacy assessment (see, for example, Fehring, 2003).

Darling-Hammond (1997) argues for learning-centered schools that are "reinventing teaching and learning" (p. 149) in ways that change both the day-to-day operations of the schools and how students, teachers, and administrators value learning. In these schools, she envisions active partnerships among teachers, students, and administrators with the primary goal of structuring rich learning experiences for all stakeholders. Similarly, partnerships between teacher preparation programs and school districts are imperative for creating learning-centered enterprises. These partnerships reform and advance the link between performance-based assessments of literacy teacher candidates and the focus on K–12 achievement data for schools.

Meiers (2003) suggests some guidelines for the creation of partnerships for literacy assessment reform at the program level. These include "signposts" (p. 177) that can help teacher preparation programs and school districts map the terrain of innovative partnerships. Briefly, these signposts include recognizing the purposes of outcome-based education, creating avenues to involve parents in assessment conversations, making assessment procedures coherent between teacher preparation programs and school districts, systematically collecting student work samples, using assessment criteria to plan instruction, and informing teaching and learning with test results. Teacher preparation programs and school districts already may be using some practices as features of their assessment plans. However, to improve literacy education and to draw upon these practices as elements of performance-based assessment for program accountability calls for a dynamic partnership. Performance-based assessment allows teacher educators to observe the process of teaching, and, by working together, schools of education and school districts can use this assessment approach to prepare teacher candidates in ways that enhance and ensure the best education for all learners.

Conclusion

Teacher preparation programs have a dual responsibility in the area of assessment that includes an obligation to both the teacher candidates and the students whom the candidates teach. Therefore, teacher preparation programs must assess teacher candidates in ways that demonstrate candidates' content knowledge of literacy as well as their understandings of assessment in real classroom situations. Teacher preparation institutions can use performance-based assessments and portfolios to ensure that teacher candidates are ready to enter diverse classrooms with content and pedagogical knowledge that they need to grow into effective literacy teachers.

Systematic assessment of teacher candidates is layered and ongoing, and it necessitates that teacher educators model the assessments that the teacher candidates are expected to learn. As teacher candidates complete their undergraduate work, it is critical that the types of assessments that are included in their course work are of the same nature as those they will be using in classrooms.

REFERENCES

Allen, M.B. (2003). *Eight questions on teacher preparation: What does the research say?* Denver, CO: Education Commission of the States.

Anders, P.L., Hoffman, J.V., & Duffy, G.G. (2000). Teaching teachers to teach reading: Paradigm shifts, persistent problems, and challenges. In M.L. Kamil, P.D. Pearson, P.B. Mosenthal, & R. Barr (Eds.), *Handbook of reading research* (Vol. 3, pp. 719–742). Mahwah, NJ: Erlbaum.

Block, C.C., Gambrell, L.B., & Pressley, M. (2002). *Improving comprehension instruction: Rethinking research, theory, and classroom practice.* San Francisco: Jossey-Bass.

Darling-Hammond, L. (1997). *Doing what matters most: Investing in quality teaching.* Sacramento: The California State University Institute for Education Reform.

Darling-Hammond, L. (2000). How teacher education matters. *Journal of Teacher Education, 51*(3), 166–173.

Davis, B., & Sumara, D.J. (1997). Cognition, complexity, and teacher education. *Harvard Educational Review, 67*(1), 105–125.

Fehring, H. (Ed.). (2003). *Literacy assessment: A collection of articles from the Australian Literacy Educators Association.* Newark, DE: International Reading Association.

Linn, R.L., & Baker, E.L. (1996). Can performance-based student assessments be psychometrically sound? In J.B. Baron & D.P. Wolf (Eds.), *Performance-based student assessment: Challenges and possibilities* (pp. 84–103). Chicago: University of Chicago Press.

Meiers, M. (2003). Assessment, reporting, and accountability in English and literacy education: Finding the signposts for the future. In H. Fehring (Ed.), *Literacy assessment: A collection of articles from the Australian Literacy Educators Association* (pp. 177–199). Newark, DE: International Reading Association.

National Council for Accreditation of Teacher Education. (1999). *A guide to college programs in teacher preparation.* San Francisco: Jossey Bass.

National Institute of Child Health and Human Development. (2000). *Report of the National Reading Panel. Teaching children to read: An evidence-based assessment of the scientific research literature on reading and its implications for reading instruction* (NIH Publication No. 00-4769). Washington, DC: U.S. Government Printing Office.

Pearson, P.D., Destefano, L., & Garcia, G. (1998). Ten dilemmas of performance assessment. In C. Harrison & T. Salinger (Eds.) *Assessing reading I: Theory and practice: International perspectives on reading assessment* (pp. 21–49). London: Routledge.

Shepard, L.A. (2000). The role of assessment in a learning culture. *Educational Researcher, 29*(7), 4–14.

Snow, C.E., Burns, M.S., & Griffin, P. (Eds.). (1998). *Preventing reading difficulties in young children.* Washington, DC: National Academy Press.

Stanovich, K.E. (2000). *Progress in understanding reading: Scientific foundations and new frontiers.* New York: Guilford.

Teacher Preparation Programs Graduate Highly Qualified Novice Teachers

NANCY FARNAN AND DANA L. GRISHAM

◆ ◆ ◆

Teacher preparation programs do not turn out teacher candidates as finished products. It takes time, learning, and practice to become an excellent teacher. Some teacher candidates learn more quickly than others, but all of them proceed along a developmental continuum in the profession. Consequently, teacher preparation programs prepare teacher candidates who are highly qualified novices—new teachers who have all of the skills and abilities to be successful teachers but who need time spent teaching to turn into master teachers. It is how we, the education establishment, treat these novices—through education and mentoring—that serves to develop and retain expert teachers.

◆ ◆ ◆

CHAPTER HIGHLIGHTS

◆ Teacher preparation must increasingly meet rigorous standards for new professionals.

◆ Teachers proceed along a developmental continuum in their profession.

◆ Initial teacher preparation programs prepare highly trained novices.

◆ Novice teachers vary in their teaching skills and knowledge.

◆ Novice teachers need solid mentoring and induction programs, or both, to extend their professional knowledge and skills.

◆ Experienced teachers need to continue their professional development throughout their careers to become "master teachers."

A WELL-PREPARED NOVICE TEACHER

Sherry, an experienced teacher in a university-based advanced credential program, talks about how she is working to become a better teacher:

> I do my teacher preparation at a state university, and actually I really feel that it is preparing me for what I need. It is teaching me the workshop model and touching on basics. I know I am learning so much more while I'm teaching. In this graduate program, I am able to gain more understanding of the theory behind some of the teaching I am doing, and I now understand my own beliefs better. I can process the learning better. I think teacher preparation is giving me some much-needed survival skills, and it is providing a foundation on which I can build my teaching. I knew how to conduct a class and teach with curriculum materials for most of my students. But now I'm learning more about how to help my struggling readers. I can't imagine not coming back [to the university] for additional professional development work in literacy.

W hat should a novice literacy teacher know and be able to do? What is appropriate teacher preparation for literacy teaching? How does experience in the profession improve literacy teaching? As literacy researchers, we have interviewed hundreds of teachers who were completing a master's degree and reading/language arts specialist credential at San Diego State University in San Diego, California, USA. These are experienced teachers who must have at least one year of teaching experience when they enter the program, but their average amount of experience in public school classrooms when they complete the program is seven and a half years. Some of these teachers seem critical of what they learned in their initial teacher preparation programs, but while interviewing them about what they have learned in their graduate classes, we have noted that their learning and experience are interwoven, and often teachers cannot explain why they "know" something and where they learned it (Grisham, 2000).

Roger (personal communication, March 15, 2004), a first-grade teacher with five years of teaching experience, explains:

> I loved the reading program because I learned so much more about comprehension strategies and was able to see it taught [in a clinic class] and understand it and take it back into my room. It's talking about the difference between the preservice program and the graduate program. With the preservice program, I don't know if I didn't get it, or maybe it was just the fact that I didn't have my own class yet, but I heard the information coming in, like, theory-wise, but I didn't apply it to anything happening in my own class. But after teaching, I knew what I needed, and so I really learned a lot in comparison.

Preparing good teachers—or in the language of the No Child Left Behind Act of 2001, "highly qualified" teachers—is a priority for universities and schools across the United States. In the 1980s various states, based on major state policy initiatives, began to include novice teacher programs in their reform efforts (see Furtwengler, 1995, for a comprehensive review of early programs). The goal of such programs was to provide ongoing teacher development and increasing teacher expertise by offering support for novice teachers through a period of induction. These programs, implemented primarily through school districts and often with the support of institutions of higher education, were designed for mentor teachers to assist and support novice teachers in their professional development (Bowers & Eberhart, 1988). Mentors or mentoring teams worked to help novice teachers hone their skills, acclimate to a particular school climate, and move toward becoming master teachers so someday they could become mentors for novices.

The acknowledgment of teacher development and the need to support it is underscored by the fact that teacher attrition, particularly in the first two or three years, has long been a problem for schools and school districts. In fact, trends in teacher attrition from 1987–2000 show that since the early 1990s, the number of teachers leaving the profession has increasingly surpassed those entering it (Darling-Hammond, 2003). Based on statistics from the Texas Center for Educational Research (2000), teacher turnover costs that state approximately $329 million a year, or $8,000 per recruit who leaves teaching. The assumption underlying novice teacher programs is that learning to teach, similar to learning skills in other disciplines, occurs in developmental stages. Primary goals of these programs are to retain new teachers in the profession (Gold, 1996) and help those teachers advance through Berliner's (1986) identified stages of competent teacher, proficient teacher, and expert teacher.

Novice Teachers vs. Expert Teachers

The journey from novice to expert has been studied and documented across various skills and disciplines. Documented differences between these stages include the level of problem-solving abilities and the breadth of strategies from which to draw for decision making. This seems to be true whether, for example, one is learning chess (Chase & Simon, 1973) or how to teach (Reynolds, 1992). Kagan's (1992) review of the literature on teacher growth supports the concept of developing expertise, particularly in the area of learning effective routines and management techniques. Grossman (1992) has concluded, after looking at numerous studies, that initial teacher preparation and credentialing "can provide frameworks for thinking about the teaching of subject matter that can influence what teachers will later learn from classroom experience" (p. 176).

The developmental perspective is so integral to thinking about teacher preparation and development that Sternberg and Horvath (1995) have called for "a reconceptualization of teaching expertise" (p. 9) that is grounded in the concept that experts differ in noteworthy ways from novices. They determine this on the premise that experts have characteristics that constitute a prototypical model of a targeted skill area, in this case teaching expertise. In other words, there are characteristics that tend to cluster and, as a group, define teaching excellence, including a strong content knowledge base, well-developed pedagogical skills, and efficient problem-solving skills. Because there are varying levels of expertise in the literacy content knowledge base, pedagogical knowledge, and the ability to solve problems in one's practice, it is important to distinguish a highly qualified novice from a "master" teacher.

The phrase *highly qualified novice* may seem to be a contradiction in terms; however, research, including a recent empirical study conducted by Laczko-Kerr and Berliner (2003) in five Arizona school districts, suggests otherwise. Teachers who graduate fully credentialed appear to teach students more effectively—if student achievement is the variable considered. Laczko-Kerr and Berliner found that students taught by uncertified teachers (those on emergency credentials with little or no professional education course work or training) had lower achievement scores on three subsets of the SAT-9 than students with fully certified teachers. They concluded that "the advantage of having a certificated teacher is worth about two months on a grade-equivalent scale" (p. 36), translating into approximately 20% of an academic year being lost for students not in those classes. This held true over the two years during which the study was conducted.

The Center for the Future of Teaching and Learning (CFTL); The California State University Institute for Education Reform; Policy Analysis for California Education; The University of California, Office of the President; and WestEd (2001) have reported similar information. The CFTL research report states that in California, the lowest performing schools have "on average 25% underprepared teachers, an increase of 2% over the past year" (n.p.). This is highly problematic for these low-performing schools attended by high percentages of minority students, especially given that, according to principals, the underprepared teachers—including interns and teachers on emergency credentials—"were less well prepared than fully credentialed recent hires" (n.p.).

In other words, it appears that there are varying degrees of expertise even at the novice level. Research also seems to support the idea that the journey from highly qualified novice to expert is, indeed, a journey. What is striking about the research on teacher preparation is the abundance of it, and one of the themes that emerges across studies on teacher growth is that different characteristics exist in novices and experts and these two stages of development are qualitatively different. Although the novice teacher who graduates from a fully certified teacher preparation program may be ready to engage productively in the teaching of children and adolescents, it seems clear that support is necessary if the new teacher is to move smoothly from novice to expert teacher. What is that support likely to be? In other words, what kinds of support do newly credentialed teachers need?

Novice Teacher Support and Development

In 1997, California legislators passed Assembly Bill 1266, which established the Beginning Teacher Support and Assessment (BTSA; 2004). Preparation for this bill had been ongoing since 1992 and was based on research from the California New Teacher Project that identified the need to provide induction support for new teachers. According to *Webster's II New Riverside Dictionary* (1996), *induction* is synonymous with *introduction* and *beginning*. To induct is "to admit as a new member: initiate." Induction, then, is the act of being inducted or initiated, and that is precisely the intention of the BTSA system—to support novice teachers by training experienced teachers to work with them in a way that fully integrates the support and formative assessment of teaching practice. These experienced teachers assist novice teachers with collecting and interpreting evidence of teaching performance, reflecting on their teaching, and identifying meaningful professional development activities that are targeted to their individual needs.

In other words, experienced teachers participate in training sessions that prepare them to mentor novice teachers effectively as they transition from initial teacher preparation and credentialing into their first years in the profession. Of interest is the early data that were collected on retention rates for first- and second-year BTSA teachers, which showed that approximately 93% remained in their classrooms in the 1999–2000 school year, with no significant differences relative to the type of school (e.g., urban vs. rural), newness of the program implementation, or the program size. Based partly on these data, the state of California funded BTSA with US$104.6 million in 2001 to accomplish the following three broad objectives: (1) to provide formative assessment of novice teachers' teaching practices and offer professional development to ensure their effectiveness with students, (2) to build teacher retention, and (3) to help ensure novice teachers' satisfaction with their profession.

In 1998, California Senate Bill (SB) 2042 was passed, representing the first major change in teacher preparation in California since the Ryan Act of 1970. Among other things, SB 2042 required that teacher preparation programs be based on standards of program quality and effectiveness that were adopted by the California Commission on Teacher Credentialing (CCTC). Therefore, in response to SB 2042, CCTC adopted new standards for teacher preparation in 2001. In addition, the CCTC adopted the Standards of Quality and Effectiveness for Professional Teacher Induction Programs in 2002. (See CCTC online at www.ctc.ca.gov for more information regarding these new standards.)

Standards for Initial Teacher Preparation vs. Teacher Induction Standards

We refer once again to California because it is one state that has fully articulated standards for initial teacher preparation as well as standards for induction in a teacher's first two years on the job. The California Standards for the Teaching Profession were originally developed through collaboration among various professional education organizations and a design team comprising of representatives from the California Department of Education (CDE), Educational Testing Services, the University of California Santa Cruz New Teacher Project, CCTC, WestEd, and others. Based on expert experience and research on best teaching practices, the standards were designed to "guide teachers as they define and develop their practice" (CCTC & CDE, 1998, p. 3).

Six categories of teacher effectiveness from the California Standards for the Teaching Profession are articulated that are relevant to initial teacher preparation (see Table 10.1). Each category represents a specific area of novice teacher performance and can be assessed by trained mentors in credential programs. Therefore, they are useful criteria for evaluating a teacher candidate's readiness to be recommended for a preliminary teaching credential.

Induction standards, relevant during a teacher's first two years on the job, focus on extending the foundational knowledge base that newly credentialed teachers bring to the classroom. These standards are monitored and evaluated during a teacher's first two years by school district–designated support providers who have the experience and expertise to mentor and support novice teachers. The requirement for induction programs to have support providers highlights the assumption that there are clear differences among mentors, support teachers (i.e., support providers), and novices embarking on their professional journeys.

Novice teachers must complete an Individual Induction Plan that builds on their foundational knowledge of teaching and learning, and they are evaluated by support providers on their abilities in the areas shown in Table 10.2. It is clear that standards for induction build on a knowledge base that novice teachers garner in their work for their preliminary credentials. The two years of mentoring during induction can only be as good as the background that novice teachers bring with them and as strong as the mentoring program. Each of the 10 areas of the Individual Induction Plan assumes a foundation of knowledge that the new teacher can expand upon. The purpose of support providers is to help new teachers build on what they

TABLE 10.1
California Standards for the Teaching Profession

1. Making subject matter comprehensible on a foundation of the state-adopted academic content standards

2. Assessing student learning, including the use of formative and summative assessments to inform instruction and assess achievement

3. Engaging and supporting students by using specialized instruction for English-language learners and developmentally appropriate teaching strategies to meet the needs of all students

4. Planning and designing instruction to ensure student achievement

5. Creating and maintaining effective learning environments, including managing instructional time and creating a positive social environment

6. Participating in ongoing development as a professional educator

California Commission on Teacher Credentialing (CCTC) & California Department of Education (CDE). (1998). *California standards for the teaching profession*. Sacramento: State of California.

TABLE 10.2
Individual Induction Plan Areas of Evaluation

1. Applying knowledge of teaching core academic content by using effective instructional practices, beyond what was exhibited in preliminary credential work

2. Reflecting on instruction and student achievement in order to ensure continuous improvement

3. Managing classrooms by setting standards for student behavior and creating a classroom climate conducive to learning for all students

4. Planning and delivering differentiated instruction for students of varying abilities, as well as for students in classrooms with cultural and linguistic diversity

5. Assessing student learning in order not only to measure student achievement, but also to inform subsequent instruction to ensure increasing achievement for all students

6. Communicating with families and communities about student progress

7. Continuing participation in professional conversations to ensure professional growth and accelerating expertise

8. Ensuring a supportive and healthy environment to ensure students' well-being and support optimal learning for all students

9. Using specialized methodologies that lead to equitable learning and achievement for students learning English as a second language

10. Using specialized knowledge and skills to provide learning opportunities for students with disabilities

California Commission on Teacher Credentialing (CCTC) & California Department of Education (CDE). (1998). *California standards for the teaching profession*. Sacramento: State of California.

know. The process of induction is most successful with a highly qualified novice. Both high-quality initial teacher preparation and a well-designed induction program are necessary.

The Continuum of Teacher Development

The United States is just beginning to recognize the need for continued mentoring and development of novice teachers. However, induction is not only a California phenomenon, nor is it found only in the United States. In Europe and Asia, educators have developed more structured systems for mentoring novice teachers (Wong, Britton, & Ganser, 2005). In their research, Britton, Paine, Pimm, and Raizen (2003) studied induction programs in the following five countries, each of which has well-funded support for all new teachers: Switzerland, Japan, France, New Zealand, and China (Shanghai). In a summary of this research, Wong and colleagues (2005) note similarities among these countries' programs. They report that the induction program in each country includes "multiple sources of assistance, typically [that] lasts at least two years, and goes beyond the imparting of mere survival skills" (p. 379).

As we have done in this chapter relative to California's induction programs, Wong and colleagues felt it was important to define *induction*, stating that it is "a highly organized and comprehensive form of staff development, involving many people and components, that typically continues as a sustained process for the first two to five years of a teacher's career" (p. 379). In the five countries studied, Wong and colleagues built all of the induction programs on several critical principles: that teachers are lifelong learners; that novice teachers are not perceived as entering the profession from a perspective of deficit, but rather must be acculturated to new professional environments via guided and mentored learning opportunities; and that induction is seen as the "initial phase of the life-long professional development of teachers" (p. 381).

Each of the principles that have been mentioned in connection with induction programs that Wong and colleagues identified fit with the model that we, the authors of this chapter, propose for a developmental continuum in teacher professional development. This model is shown in Figure 10.1. The model reflects the view that initial teacher preparation programs provide a foundation on which the highly qualified novice may build. Through a well-designed induction program, the teacher grows as a professional with mentoring and support from more knowledgeable peers

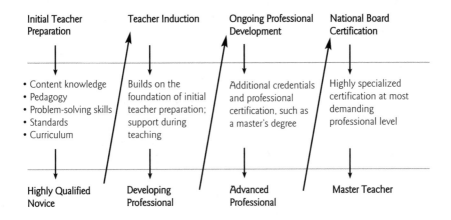

FIGURE 10.1
Teacher Developmental Continuum

Initial Teacher Preparation

Teacher Induction

Ongoing Professional Development

National Board Certification

• Content knowledge
• Pedagogy
• Problem-solving skills
• Standards
• Curriculum

Builds on the foundation of initial teacher preparation; support during teaching

Additional credentials and professional certification, such as a master's degree

Highly specialized certification at most demanding professional level

Highly Qualified Novice

Developing Professional

Advanced Professional

Master Teacher

(support providers). After induction, teachers may earn advanced professional status through ongoing professional development activities, such as university programs for additional certification (for example, the reading/language arts specialist credential in California); advanced degrees, such as a master's degree; or well-designed district-level professional development programs in literacy or other content areas. A novice teacher becomes a master teacher when he or she earns the prestigious national board certification in literacy or another content area.

Conclusion

Robin (personal communication, March 15, 2004), a second-year teacher at an urban school, talked to us about the benefits of her induction program:

> I wouldn't have made it without Nora, an induction support provider. She helped me plan lessons that would meet the needs of the English learners in my classroom. That was really great, because I sort of knew what I needed to do, but it helped to have someone who actually had the experience. She really got down to the details and supported me as I tried things.

Robin outlined how this interaction with a more knowledgeable peer (a designated support provider) helped her in other ways as well—taking her place in the classroom so Robin could observe more experienced teachers with their students, helping Robin evaluate some of her students' work to make more informed instructional decisions, showing Robin more effective ways to group her students and differentiate instruction, and initiating Robin into the culture of teaching in her school.

Robin is more fortunate than many novice teachers who find themselves alone and teaching in some of the toughest teaching assignments around the United States. To cultivate good teachers, the education profession needs excellent undergraduate education and high-quality teacher preparation programs that unite theory and practice. We need, as well, to recognize that teachers grow in their profession as they gain experience, thereby grounding and expanding their initial expertise. Mentoring and induction programs can strengthen and expand their knowledge base. In the teaching profession, we need to conceptualize a developmental continuum for teachers just as we do for other professions and trades. Only when teachers gain a strong foundation for teaching, continue their development with a sound and rigorous induction program, return to the university for curriculum-based graduate training and/or a master's degree, and then work to earn National Board Certification can they truly be called *master teachers*.

REFERENCES

Beginning Teacher Support and Assessment (BTSA). (2004). *Beginning Teacher Support and Assessment—Basics*. Retrieved April 21, 2005, from http://www.btsa.ca.gov/BTSA_basics.html

Berliner, D.C. (1986). In pursuit of the expert pedagogue. *Educational Researcher, 15*(7), 5–13.

Bowers, G.R., & Eberhart, N.A. (1988). Mentors and the entry-year program. *Theory Into Practice, 27*(3), 226–230.

Britton, E., Paine, L., Pimm, D., & Raizen, S. (Eds.). (2003). *Comprehensive teacher induction: Systems for early career learning*. Dordrecht, Netherlands: Kluwer Academic Publishers; San Francisco: West Ed.

California Commission on Teacher Credentialing (CCTC). (2002). *Standards of quality and effectiveness for professional teacher induction programs*. Sacramento: State of California.

California Commission on Teacher Credentialing (CCTC) & California Department of Education (CDE). (1998). *California standards for the teaching profession*. Sacramento: State of California.

Center for the Future of Teaching and Learning (CFTL); The California State University Institute for Education Reform; Policy Analysis for California Education; The University of California, Office of the President; & WestEd. (2001). *The status of the teaching profession 2001*. Santa Cruz, CA: Center for the Future of Teaching and Learning. Retrieved May 9, 2005, from http://www.cftl.org/documents/2001CFTLpwrpnt.pdf

Chase, W.G., & Simon, H.A. (1973). Perception in chess. *Cognitive Psychology, 4*, 55–81.

Darling-Hammond, L. (2003). Keeping good teachers: Why it matters, what leaders can do. *Education Leadership, 60*(8), 6–13.

Furtwengler, C.B. (1995, February 15). Beginning teachers programs: Analysis of state actions during the reform era. *Education Policy Analysis Archives, 3*(3). Retrieved April 22, 2005, from http://epaa.asu.edu/epaa/v3n3.html

Gold, Y. (1996). Beginning teacher support: Attrition, mentoring, and induction. In J. Sikula, T.J. Buttery, & E. Guyton (Eds.), *Handbook of research on teacher education* (2nd ed., pp. 548–594). New York: Macmillan.

Grisham, D.L. (2000). Connecting theoretical conceptions of reading to practice: A longitudinal study of elementary school teachers. *Reading Psychology, 21*(2), 145–170.

Grossman, P.L. (1992). Why models matter: An alternative view on professional growth in teaching. *Review of Educational Research, 62*(2), 171–179.

Kagan, D.M. (1992). Professional growth among preservice and beginning teachers. *Review of Educational Research, 62*(2), 129–169.

Laczko-Kerr, I., & Berliner, D.C. (2003). In harm's way: How undercertified teachers hurt their students. *Educational Leadership, 60*(8), 34–39.

No Child Left Behind Act of 2001, Pub. L. No. 107-110, 115 Stat. 1425 (2002).

Reynolds, A. (1992). What is competent beginning teaching? A review of the literature. *Review of Educational Research, 62*(1), 1–35.

Sternberg, R.J., & Horvath, J.A. (1995). A prototype view of expert teaching. *Educational Researcher, 24*(6), 9–17.

Texas Center for Educational Research. (2000). *The cost of teacher turnover.* Austin: Texas State Board for Teacher Certification.

Webster's II New Riverside Dictionary (rev. ed.). (1996). Boston: Houghton Mifflin.

Wong, H.K., Britton, T., & Ganser, T. (2005). What the world can teach us about new teacher induction. *Phi Delta Kappan, 86*(5), 379–384.

CONCLUSION

The Truth About Literacy Teacher Preparation

SUSAN DAVIS LENSKI, DANA L. GRISHAM, AND LINDA S. WOLD

L iteracy teacher preparation often is misunderstood by the public and policymakers and is, therefore, beginning to be criticized just as K–12 educators have been for so long. In an article about the history of literacy education, Pearson (2004) writes,

> After a decade of laying the blame for the ills of U.S. education at the feet of teachers, reformers have shifted the blame to teacher educators, who get blamed for just about every problem in U.S. education and many in U.S. society. (p. 4)

However, many people who foster a negative view of literacy teacher preparation are reacting to ideas from the past. According to Goodlad (2002), "The renewal of teacher education is hindered like no other field by myths derived from yesterday's knowledge made credible by mandated policies" (p. 218). As a field, however, literacy education must move beyond the myths of the past to the truths of the present. During the past two decades, teacher preparation has made impressive changes and has developed a solid research base.

During our extensive review of research, we found that teacher preparation research remains both rigorous and relevant, albeit mostly in high-quality, small-scale individual studies. The evidence presented in this volume can add to the knowledge base of the truths that surround literacy teacher preparation research. In every one of the 10 truths, we found strong data that represented a range of research that grounds teaching and learning in teacher preparation. Rather than regarding teacher preparation as "the problem" in education policy, teacher accountability, and student achievement levels, we argue that teacher preparation programs are part of the solution. In many literacy teacher preparation programs, literacy teacher educators take on a complex and crucial endeavor—that of helping college students transform themselves into committed and passionate literacy teaching professionals who are willing to work toward enhanced intellectual growth and strategic practice.

Although we found that literacy teacher preparation has a reputable research base, we also found that it is imperative to continue conducting quality research to answer the most pressing questions involving the preparation of literacy teachers. In addition, we believe it is important to disseminate the research findings that are available and to educate literacy teacher candidates about the importance of using research to guide their decision making. The graduates of literacy teacher preparation programs are the teachers of tomorrow. We believe it is important for these new literacy teachers to recognize how evidence-based research should be the foundation for classroom practices.

The examination of these 10 truths in literacy teacher preparation provides important evidence of the improved quality of literacy teacher preparation. These advances are due to the energy and expertise of teacher educators and literacy teacher preparation researchers. As many professionals do, literacy teacher educators are becoming more knowledgeable about the field, which includes the preparation of future teachers and learning what makes good teaching (Tell, 2001). In this volume, our focus has been to help the public understand and envision the quality of literacy teachers' intellectual work within literacy teaching practices and the research base that exists about literacy teacher preparation. The research of literacy teaching continues and the knowledge base continues to grow. As literacy preparation programs respond to the growing body of research, literacy teacher candidates will become even better prepared for teaching literacy to generations to come.

REFERENCES

Goodlad, J.I. (2002). Teacher education research: The outside and the inside. *Journal of Teacher Education, 53*(3), 216–221.

Pearson, P.D. (2001). Learning to teach reading: The status of the knowledge base. In C.M. Roller (Ed.), *Learning to teach reading: Setting the research agenda* (pp. 4–19). Newark, DE: International Reading Association.

Tell, C. (2001). Appreciating good teaching: A conversation with Lee Shulman. *Educational Leadership, 58*(5), 6–11.

APPENDIX

Additional Internet Resources on Literacy Education and Teacher Preparation

This appendix provides Internet resources for referencing more detailed information related to the 10 truths. Those interested in literacy education advocacy and teacher preparation research may find the websites useful as starting points for learning more about and becoming enthusiastic supporters of excellence in literacy teacher preparation.

American Association of Colleges for Teacher Education (AACTE)
www.aacte.org

California Commission on Teacher Credentialing (CCTC)
www.ctc.ca.gov

Carnegie Corporation of New York
www.carnegie.org

Center on Education Policy (CEP)
www.cep-dc.org

Center for the Study of Teaching and Policy (CTP)
http://depts.washington.edu/ctpmail

Education Commission of the States (ECS)
http://ecs.org

International Reading Association (IRA)
www.reading.org

International Reading Association's Standards for Reading Professionals
www.reading.org/resources/issues/reports/professional_standards.html

Literacy Teacher Preparation: Ten Truths Teacher Educators Need to Know by Susan Davis Lenski, Dana L. Grisham, and Linda S. Wold, Editors. Copyright © 2006 by the International Reading Association.

Interstate New Teacher Assessment and Support Consortium (INTASC)
www.ccsso.org/projects/interstate_new_teacher_assessment_and_support_
consortium

National Board for Professional Teaching Standards (NBPTS)
www.nbpts.org

National Center for Education Information (NCEI)
www.ncei.com

National Center for Education Statistics (NCES)
http://nces.ed.gov

The National Commission on Excellence in Elementary Teacher Preparation for Reading Instruction
www.reading.org/resources/issues/reports/teacher_education.html

National Commission on Teaching and America's Future (NCTAF)
www.nctaf.org

National Council for Accreditation of Teacher Education (NCATE)
www.ncate.org

National Council of Teachers of English (NCTE)
www.ncte.org

National Reading Panel (NRP)
www.nationalreadingpanel.org

No Child Left Behind Act (NCLB)
www.ed.gov/nclb

Texas Center for Educational Research (TCER)
www.tcer.org

U.S. Department of Education Reading First
www.ed.gov/programs/readingfirst

INDEX

Page numbers followed by *f* or *t* indicate figures or tables, respectively.

A

AACTE. *See* American Association of Colleges for Teacher Education
ABDAL-HAQQ, I., 21, 58, 62, 73–74
AC PROGRAMS. *See* alternative certification programs
ACCOUNTABILITY: national, 68–69; school-level, 71–72; state-level, 69–71
ADSIT, J.N., 36, 41
ADVANCED PROFESSIONALS, 111*f*
ADVANCEMENTS, 60–61
AFRICAN AMERICANS, 50
ALLEN, M.B., 16, 19–20, 76, 90, 96, 100
ALLINGTON, R.L., 68, 75
ALTERNATIVE CERTIFICATION PROGRAMS, 86
ALTERNATIVE ROUTE (AR) PROGRAMS. *See* alternative teacher preparation programs
ALTERNATIVE TEACHER PREPARATION PROGRAMS, 76–91; alignment with traditional teacher preparation, 87–89; effect on education policy, 86; inconsistencies in, 85; issues related to, 84–86; positive findings, 86–87; quality programs, 83–87, 88*t*, 88–89; research on, 86–87; resources on advantages of, 79, 80*t*–82*t*
AMERICAN ASSOCIATION OF COLLEGES FOR TEACHER EDUCATION (AACTE), 34–36, 41, 116
ANDERS, P.L., 4, 9, 11, 56–57, 60, 62, 96, 100
ANDERSON, R., 56, 62
ANTHONY, E., 16–17, 19–20
APPLEBEE, A.N., 36–37, 41
APPRENTICESHIP, 78
AR (ALTERNATIVE ROUTE) PROGRAMS. *See* alternative teacher preparation programs
ARCHIBALD, G., 80*t*
ASH, G.E., 74–75

ASHLEY, C., 4, 11, 49, 52
ASSESSMENT, 79; informal, 93; literacy, 38; of literacy teachers, 94–95; performance-based model, 97–98, 98–99; program, 96–97; purpose of, 92–101; Reading Instruction Competence Assessment (RICA), 71; Standard 5: Effective Curriculum, Teaching, and Assessment Practices (California), 70; with students, 93; systematic, 100; of teacher candidates, 96–97; in teacher preparation programs, 92–101
AU, K.H., 60, 62
AUTONOMY, 79

B

BAINES, L., 38, 41
BAKER, E.L., 95, 100
BALLENTINE, D., 4, 12
BARR, R., 4, 11–12
BEACH, D., 81*t*, 88*t*, 89–90
BEAN, T.W., 4, 11
BEGINNING TEACHER SUPPORT AND ASSESSMENT (BTSA), 107, 112
BEGORAY, D.L., 39, 41
BELL, J., viii, xiv
BERGERON, B.S., 75
BERLINER, D.C., viii, xiv, 27, 31, 80*t*–82*t*, 83, 87, 90, 105–106, 112–113
BERRY, B., 81*t*, 85, 88*t*, 90
BIDDLE, B.J., viii, xiv
BLOCK, C.C., 94, 100
BOLES, K.C., 66, 75
BOWERS, G.R., 104, 112
BRINK, B., 60, 62, 75
BRITTON, E., 110, 112
BRITTON, T., 113
BRITZMAN, D.P., 35, 41

methodological considerations, 6–10; reading research war, 38; reasonable conclusions, 9–10; on teacher preparation programs, 17

RESEARCH QUESTIONS, 7–8

RESOURCES, 78; additional Internet resources, 116–117; on advantages of traditional and alternative route programs, 79, 80t–82t; on components of quality alternative route programs, 88, 88t

RESPONSIBLE PRACTICE STANDARDS, 18

RESPONSIVE INSTRUCTION, 67–72

RESTA, V., 80t, 84, 88t, 91

REYNOLDS, A., 105, 113

RICA. See Reading Instruction Competence Assessment

RIGOR: definition of, 24; in literacy assessment courses, 27–30; in literacy course work, 22–31; in literacy teaching, 25–27; recognition of, 27; teaching, 30

ROBERTSON, STEPHANIE, 90

ROLLER, C.M., 5, 12, 17, 20

ROSEMARY, C.A., 4, 12

ROTHENBERG, J., 58, 62

ROTHERDAM, J.A., 39, 42

RUDENGA, E., 83–84

S

SAILORS, M.W., 11

SAN DIEGO STATE UNIVERSITY, 69, 104

SCHERER, M., 85, 91

SCHOENFELD, A.H., 4, 11

SCHOOL CURRICULA, 64–76

SCHOOL-LEVEL ACCOUNTABILITY, 71–72

SCHWARTZ, H., 20–21

SCOTT, J., 56, 62

SHEPARD, L.A., 95, 101

SHORT, K.G., ix, xiv, 37, 42

SHULMAN, L.S., 47, 52, 57, 60, 62

SIGNPOSTS, 99

SIMMONS, J., 34, 43

SIMON, H.A., 105, 112

SLAVIN, R.E., 37, 43

SMITH, C., 66, 75

SMITH, K., 34, 39, 43

SMITH, M.W., 37, 42

SMITH, N.B., 56, 62

SNOW, C.E., 9, 12, 94, 101

SNYDER, J., 42

SPECIALLY DESIGNED ACADEMIC INSTRUCTION IN ENGLISH STRATEGIES, 66

SPIEGEL, H.A.L., 37, 43

STANDARD 3 (COLORADO DEPARTMENT OF EDUCATION), 69–70

STANDARD 5: EFFECTIVE CURRICULUM, TEACHING, AND ASSESSMENT PRACTICES (CALIFORNIA), 70

STANDARDS: for initial teacher preparation, 108–110; link with literacy curriculum, 71; for novice teacher candidates, 25–26; professional, 18–19, 27–30; for responsible practice, 18; for rigor in literacy teaching, 25–27; for teacher candidates, 17–19; teacher induction, 108–110; teacher preparation, 69–70, 72. See also specific standards by name

STANDARDS FOR QUALITY AND EFFECTIVENESS FOR PROFESSIONAL TEACHER INDUCTION, 107

STANDARDS FOR READING PROFESSIONALS (IRA), 117

STANDARDS FOR READING PROFESSIONALS—REVISED 2003 (IRA), 26–27

STANDARDS OF THE ENGLISH LANGUAGE ARTS (IRA & NCTE), 60

STANOVICH, K.E., 38, 43, 94, 101

STATE-LEVEL ACCOUNTABILITY, 69–71

STEINMETZ, L., 12

STEPHENS, D., 27, 31

STERNBERG, R.J., 105, 113

STOCK, P.L., 34, 39, 43

STRICKLAND, D.S., 36, 43

STUDENTS: diversity among, 37; informal assessment with, 93; literacy needs of, 50–51; teacher preparation, teacher certification, and, 19

SUMARA, D.J., 94, 100

SUMSION, J., 49, 52

SUPPORT FOR NOVICE TEACHERS, 107

SWITZER, T.J., 20–21

SWITZERLAND, 110

SYSTEMATIC ASSESSMENT, 100

SYSTEMWIDE EVALUATION OF PROFESSIONAL TEACHER PREPARATION PROGRAMS: AN INITIATIVE OF THE

blank page